D1245315

YOU CAN'T
FLY TO
HEAVEN IN A
STRAIGHT
LINE

YOU CAN'T FLY TO HEAVEN IN A STRAIGHT LINE

MARVIN PHILLIPS

HOWARD
PUBLISHING CO.

3117 North 7th
West Monroe, Louisiana 71291

The purpose of Howard Publishing is threefold:

*Inspiring** holiness in the lives of believers,

*Instilling** hope in the hearts of struggling people everywhere,

*Instructing** believers toward a deeper faith in Jesus Christ,
Because he's coming again.

Howard Publishers
3117 North 7th Street, West Monroe, LA 71291-2227

Printed in the United States of America

Third Printing 1991

ISBN# 1-878990-02-0

DEDICATION

*To Dot whose loyalty is my greatest asset,
and whose love is my greatest joy!*

Contents

Contents

Introduction

You Can't Fly to Heaven in a Straight Line is a fast-paced, hard-hitting, uplifting, image-building, God-honoring message that is aimed directly at you. The book is broken down into a number of categories and each category has pertinent, useable, and inspiring information. Marvin Phillips has captured the spirit of God's message in a manner that will be of interest and benefit to everyone. The advice is practical, and it definitely offers hope to the reader. At this time, America and Americans—and for that matter, the world—are in need of this priceless ingredient called "hope." It's a book on faith, but it is not "preachy." It is a book chock-full of sentence sermons, but it is not the least bit stuffy. By no stretch of the imagination could you call it a humorous book, and yet there are those moments and instances where you will smile at your good fortune for having picked it

up to read. It is a book you will want to read
and then read again. More importantly, you will
want to take the action that Marvin Phillips so
beautifully advocates.

Zig Ziglar

CHAPTER ONE

You Can't Fly to Heaven
In a Straight Line!

She sat in my office, hands clasped together in
her lap. She had that dejected pose: head down,
back bent slightly forward, and the defeat fairly
whined in her voice. "I just can't make it. I try
so hard, but I just can't stay up, like all you Christians do."

What is it about us that we think we are so
different? We think everybody else is always
happy, always up, always positive. We think no
one faces problems, hardships, setbacks, and diffi-
culties but us! Our case must be unusual; we were
just born different. That's it, we were just born
different!

But after years in the ministry and after hearing
all kinds of human problems and situations, I am
convinced that if we all confessed all our fears,
weaknesses, and sins to each other, we would
laugh at each other for our lack of originality.

Friend, we are all pretty much alike. No one
stays up all the time. We do not make it in life
because we are superior, and we do not fail because

we are inferior. Success is a process and happiness is a skill. This book is to give you good news. Anyone can make it who will just pay attention to the rules. But, as the title of this book suggests, "You Can't Fly to Heaven in a Straight Line."

Suppose you and I board a jet plane bound for New York. After a few moments of what seems to be routine flying, our pilot's voice comes on the intercom and says, "Folks, this is your pilot. I have a terrible confession to make. When we took off from Tulsa, I had every intention of flying you good people to New York. I aimed this great plane in the right direction, but I just keep drifting off course. I must confess that this has happened to me many times before, but I told myself that this time would be different. I guess I'm just not cut out to be a pilot. I'm going to do my best to get you back to Tulsa. From there you can either catch another plane or get to New York the best way you can. I'm so sorry."

Now brothers and sisters, I don't mind telling you, that little conversation would unnerve me just a bit. I mean, if your pilot isn't confident and qualified, you ain't got much, and that's for sure.

But then the voice of the copilot comes on and saves the day. He says, "Folks, you've got nothing to worry about. I've made this journey many times before. Everything your pilot said was true, but you see, because of the curve of the earth, and the changes in the direction of the wind, we are constantly flying off course. All we do is set our course for New York, and with all these million-dollar instruments, we just make a few adjustments now and then, and that's the way we get to New York from Tulsa every day of the year. You just relax and have a good time. We'll have you in New York right on schedule, just like the book says." I feel better already!

Hey, neighbor, don't you realize you can't get anywhere in a straight line. There are turns, curves and adjustments that must be made along the trip; and in the end, the expected destination is reached.

Where Do You Really Want to Go?

Your goal, your final destination, must be fixed in your mind. Without it you are as lost as our pilot friend. Whether we are talking about a plane trip, your job, your marriage, or your church, it is important to get firmly fixed in your mind where you really want to go. Then, with that decision prayerfully made, you begin to take the steps and make the adjustments that get you there.

Let's take a simple illustration. My wife and I moved into a lovely home in Northeast Tulsa about eleven miles from the church where I preach. Whenever I go from the church building to my home—counting all the turns and curves, even the short ones—here's about what happens. I leave the parking lot headed due east. My first turn is north. Then I turn east again before I get on an interstate highway, which curves from northeast to due north. I finally leave this highway and make another turn east. Then I travel a short way west, make three or four shorter turns, and find myself parked in my driveway, now headed south.

Now, put like that, it sounds like a harrowing,

nerve-racking experience; when in reality it is a lovely enjoyable trip. I end up reaching my destination and achieving my goal. There just isn't any way to get from my church building to my house by traveling in a straight line. And it is physically impossible to travel from Tulsa to New York in a straight line.

Come to think of it, you can't reach emotional goals, job goals, financial goals, or even spiritual goals in a straight line either. The ultimate goal must be set, and many adjustments must be made before you arrive where you really want to be.

Back to that pathetic lady in my office. She assumed that other people never have any "downs." She supposed that they are always happy, always strong, and always know who they are and where they are going. And the truth is, my friend, there just "ain't no such animal."

A "Straight Line" Would Be Boring!

Come to think of it, the most common cause of wrecks on some of our turnpikes is boredom. People actually get tired of the straight roads. The reflectors on the median strip have a hypnotic effect, and pretty soon, the tired driver is asleep and tragedy often follows.

This is not so on the course that has hills, turns, and changes of scenery. This kind of road is much more scenic, exposes you to more beauty, and indeed is more restful. Just as it is on an automobile trip, so it is in life.

Problems sharpen our senses and appeal to our

sense of challenge. I'd go so far as to say that without them we'd be pretty much in the same condition as that hypnotized driver on the straight freeway . . . bored, tired, and headed for trouble.

There Are Adjustments in Life!

It is a foregone conclusion that you have what it takes to make the necessary adjustments in life. The Bible says you've been created in the image of God. You've been designed to succeed and to enjoy this old earth that God made especially for you. The challenges will sharpen your senses, the problems will call forth your best thinking, and the setbacks will put strength in your backbone. Through it all, you'll learn and achieve. God wants you to "live life to the full" (John 10:10).

What This Book Is All About!

What follows on these succeeding pages are exciting things that were taught in a recent course in Columbus Elementary School in Tulsa. It was called, "Christian Mental Attitude." It shows God's plan for you and how you can meet life head on and have the time of your life. Trust the One who made you in His Image. He doesn't make junk!

CHAPTER TWO

I Am Loveable and Capable

I must tell you that I begin each of my classes in this course by having all the students stand and repeat after me at the top of their voices:

I am Made in God's Image . . .
I can Choose my Attitude
I Choose to Feel Great!

There are several reasons why we do this. First, because it is true! Second, because having thus encouraged each other, we are in a much better frame of mind to listen to the positive things that will be taught in the class. And third, we must realize that we all have choices. That great power of choice will be discussed in a later chapter.

I'm sure you all thought you were born naked! But the truth is, you were born with a big, wide ribbon wrapped all around you! On the ribbon was a sign that said, *"I am loveable and capable!"* Our greatest battle in life is to keep that sign intact! But we have unbelievable help in ripping it to shreds.

Have you paid any attention to babies! It is obvious they all still have their sign. They believe in themselves! They think they are irresistible to everybody else, and they generally are! They think they can do anything. Now the reason they think this is because they are newly created, and God gave them this self-confidence—this healthy self-esteem. And that's the way we humans are supposed to live our entire lives. But along comes a thoughtless momma, who says, "You always look a mess," and there goes a little bit of our sign. "You'll be the death of me yet," and another piece of the sign comes tearing off. Other negative gems: are "Can't you do anything right?" "You're lying to me," "That was a stupid thing to do," or how about this one, "I told you so!"

Man, we're lucky if we make it through high school with our sign as large as a postage stamp.

Oh, now and then we get a piece of our sign pasted back on. Someone says, "Hey, you did great," and we can piece back a little bit of the sign. Or, "I'm proud of you," and another piece of the sign goes back on.

Come to think of it, friend, how does your sign look? And just as important, what do you do to the other fellow's sign?

Who Am I, Anyway?

On the first page of the Bible we read that we were created in the image of God. That makes us "exclusive!" And you know how we humans love exclusives! A woman will pay anything for a

dress that is "exclusive." If she sees another woman
with a dress just like it, the dress immediately
becomes "a cheap old thing."

Well, human beings are the only things in the
universe created in God's image. And there are
no two human beings *exactly alike*. Even identical
twins are not alike in every way. Someone said,
"No two people are exactly alike; and both of them
are proud of it."

But there's not another human being in the
whole world exactly like you. You are an original!
There will never be another person just like you.

And We Are "Wonderfully Made"

It's probably best that God made us. If I had
made man, I would have made him a whole lot
different. I would have put his eyes on the ends
of his fingers. That way, he could look around a
corner without anyone seeing him. I would have
put an eye in the back of his head for "reverse
seeing." Of course, he would be in trouble when
he shampooed his hair, wouldn't he?

David said in the Psalms, "I am wonderfully
made!" Years ago man invented the camera. It
was a big, bulky thing that didn't do a very good
job, but in time there were improvements. Black
and white gave way to color. Then there were shut-
ter speeds, lens openings, fast focus, flash, and
then came those instant cameras that spit out
pictures into your hands and developed them before your eyes. Marvelous thing!

God put a camera in the first man he ever made. It had color, instant focus, full range, and even repaired itself. My, but you are "fearfully and wonderfully made." You are really something!

Then man invented the telegraph, and that was really something. Through insulated wires, man could then send and receive messages which were tapped out in morse code.

When God created the first man, he created him with a completely modern telegraph that will never be improved upon. When your hand touches a hot stove, it instantly sends a message to the brain. The message travels through all those nerves, saying "Ouch, this thing is hot." Then the brain sends back a message faster than a split-second, "You fool, get your hand off that stove."

Are you getting the point, my friend? What we're saying is that you are something special. There is nothing in creation to compare with a human being like you. It just wouldn't make any sense at all to conclude that we are all made in God's image, and then to suppose that God wanted his creation to be *mediocre!*

"I Read the Last Page"

I confess to you that I did something that perhaps I shouldn't have. I was reading there in the Bible about how God made us and how we should live life to the fullest. But I read about all the weaknesses, problems, obstacles, and sins that would beset us. Then I sneaked a look at the last page . . . and what do you know—*we won!* Since I know how it all comes out, I'm not going to be "hung up" and inhibited about life now. I will live it to the fullest, knowing that the victory belongs to those who have read the book, who know the author, and who put themselves in his hands!

CHAPTER THREE

Choose Your Way to Success

Slatsville Junior College decided to upgrade its image. They decided that every member of the faculty and administration should have a doctor's degree, and that every employee of the college should have at least a bachelor's degree. Well they found one janitor that not only didn't have a degree, but who couldn't even read and write—so they promptly fired him.

But he was a positive thinker. He took what savings he had and bought an old dump truck and began hauling for a living. He did pretty good at it. And before long, he had to buy a second truck, and then a third. Then he bought a new one and another and again another.

He finally approached his banker and said, "Bob, I've got to have a million dollar loan to expand my business." The banker replied, "Tom, it's a pleasure to do business with you. Your trucking business is a credit to this community. You hire a lot of people, and do a great business. My board has instructed me to lend you the million dollars. I've already prepared the papers. All you have to do is sign the loan and the million dollars is yours."

Tom said, "Bob, I hate to tell you this, I really do, but I can't read and write. You're going to have to witness my X on that loan." This just blew the banker's mind. "You mean you've done all this without even being able to read and write? Where would you be if you'd had an education?" And Tom replied, "I'd be *janitor* at Slatsville Junior College!"

The lesson is infinitely clear, isn't it? It's not whether you are male or female; it's not whether you've been born with a silver spoon in your mouth; it's what you do with what you've got that counts. That's what really zooms you to the top or sinks you to the bottom.

My First Positive Thinking Rally

I remember attending my first Positive Thinking Rally some years ago. Things weren't going right, and I was down at the time. Someone suggested going to Kansas City to hear Paul Harvey, Zig Ziglar, Cavet Robert, and others. Well I really didn't want to go, but my wife said, "Marvin, I wish you'd go. You're not too easy to live with just now. I think it would do you good, and besides, I need the rest." Well I went! And I'm so glad I did!

I heard all these famous motivators saying "You can do what you want to do; you can go where you want to go, and you can have anything you want to have." They said, "It isn't the size or even the number of problems you have, it's what you do about those problems that counts." Oh man, this really made sense. I don't mind telling you it completely turned my life around.

The Bible: Original Handbook on Positive Thinking!

Being a preacher, it didn't take me long to realize I could put book, chapter, and verse to everything those speakers were saying. Didn't the apostle Paul say, "I can do all things through Christ which strengthens me" (Phil. 4:13). Didn't Solomon say, "As a man thinks in his heart, so is he!" (Prov. 23:7). And remember those fantastic words of Jesus, "all things are possible to the man who believes" (Mark 9:23).

Let me illustrate it this way. My son bought a new car a few years back. For some reason, which I've forgotten, he asked me to go downtown and drive it home. It was a Pinto, you know, one of those small things. Some cars you get into—this one you "put on." If you have carburetor trouble, you throw it over your shoulder and burp it.

Anyway, I got it home and drove it into the driveway, but I couldn't turn off the ignition. Now I was amused, because after all, it was new and stiff and you probably had to jiggle it. So I jiggled it! But I still couldn't get the key turned off. Well it was a "four-on-the-floor" job, so I reasoned that I could push in the clutch, put my foot on the brake, put it in first gear, let out the clutch, and the motor would die. Well I got all that done. The engine was off, but I still couldn't get the key out. Now I was really upset! Of all the cars in the world, this was probably the only one that you couldn't get the key out of the lock. Ford Motor Company had sold my boy a lemon.

I was working up all sorts of things against the system, including believing the Communists were behind this plot. Then I had a flash of genius. I looked in the glove compartment, whipped out the owner's manual and looked under "I" for Ignition (no, not for Idiot!). It read, "On the left side of the steering column there is a button. Depress the button, and the key will come out!"

All this time I had been bad-mouthing the manu-facturers, but they had been doing some thinking on their own. They were saying "We want this boy to enjoy this car. We don't want anyone to steal it, so we'll put on an anti-theft device."

It was some time later when I got the real lesson. You see, your Bible is like that. God has made you with all those organs you can see, and all the stuff inside you can't see. He put all those feelings, drives, and desires in you. Then he wrote a book (your owner's manual if you please) to tell you how to understand and use all that good stuff. It's like a sign I saw once on the side of a compli-cated computor, "When all else fails, read the in-structions."

God's Greatest Gift to You

All sorts of people will read this book, and I surely hope you'll recommend it to others. We all have one thing in common; we all have "choice." It's a pity that some don't know this. They say, "I had no choice." But ladies and gentlemen, there is never a time that you don't have choice, and choice is God's greatest gift to you. You can use your choice to be, do, or have anything you want.

Choice Is More Important Than Fact!

What you do about what happens to you is more important than what happens to you! Your attitude, more than your aptitude, determines your altitude!

I have a daughter in college. When she was a sophomore in High School, one night she said to me, "Dad, tomorrow is going to be a rough day." I said, "Tam, why is tomorrow going to be so bad?" She said, "Well I broke up with my boyfriend tonight, and he has that rare ability to intimidate me. He makes everything seem my fault. His locker is next to mine at school, and I'll bump into him between every class. He'll give me a rough time all day long. I wish I could just take tomorrow and rip it off the calendar."

I said, "Wait a minute, Tam. Everyone wakes up every morning with two lists; on one list you've got 'reasons to be glad,' and on the other, 'reasons to be sad.'"

Now here's a strange thing. You never see anyone who is "glad-sad" do you? You never ask anybody, "How are you doing today?" and have them reply "super-terrible." I mean, they're either one or the other. And that's strange since we all have both lists. It must be because we have the power to choose which "list" we're going to emphasize.

I encouraged Tammy to emphasize her good list.

She said, "What do you mean, my 'good list'?" So
I answered, "How about the fact that you have a
mom and dad who love each other; and they love
you. You have a good home, we have enough money
to buy everything we need. You have your youth,
your health, and you have the Lord Jesus in your
life." Tammy thought it was worth a try to emphasize these things for a day. At the end of the day
I asked her, "Hey, Tam, how'd your day go?" She
said, "Dad, you're not going to believe this. It went
fantastic."

My reading friend, could I ask you a question?
Since you also have both lists, how are things going
in your life?

One Man's Limp, Another Man's Leap!

Many of you will remember Tom Dempsey. He
made it all the way to the top. He played football
for the New Orleans' Saints, and for some time
his 63-yard field goal was a world record, despite
the fact that he had only one hand . . . and *no
toes* on his kicking foot.

The most exhilarating book in the Bible is the
little book of Philippians. It only has four chapters.
You can read it in 10 minutes. In it, Paul wrote
some exciting words, "Rejoice in the Lord. Let me
say it again, Rejoice; don't worry about anything,
pray about everything. And the peace of God that
passes understanding, shall keep your hearts and
minds in Christ Jesus" (Phil. 4:4–6). How would
you like to feel like that?

You say, man, Paul lived a long time ago. He

never had to pay $600.00 a month house payment; Paul never paid $300.00 a month car payment. He never had to buy $1.50 per gallon gasoline. Man, if Paul had the problems we have in the twentieth century, he wouldn't be saying "everybody be happy."

But then, maybe you don't know that when Paul wrote those words he was at that moment in a Roman jail awaiting execution. If you interviewed Paul, he would likely say, "I've got two lists. I am happy 'because of my hope in Christ; and I'm happy in spite of being in prison." You see, one man's limp really is another man's leap.

Use "Choice" to Get What You Want!

Our problem in achievement is not that we lack opportunity or ability—it is "choice." Someone said that we "aim at nothing, and then achieve it with remarkable accuracy."

Garson L. Rice, Greensboro, North Carolina, made headlines by making a world's record: 904 Toyotas in a single month. In the newspaper interview he said some significant things.

Business wasn't always good for Rice. Twelve years ago when he started, he sold only 120 cars the whole year. His financial backing pulled out on him; folks told him he was crazy for selling those cars made in "Jay-pan!" But Garson L. Rice *persisted!* And twelve years later when he broke the world's record in sales, they were all surprised . . . all, that is, except Garson Rice, because you see, he *expected* to break it. More than that, he *concentrated* on ways to get his product into the hands of the people. He claimed that this kind of thinking had to be deeper than the usual "coffee table" planning sessions. "You've got to agonize over it," he said. Mr. Rice believes in *enthusiasm.* His salesmen are among the most excited and enthused in the world. He believes you can sell what you're sold on. Then came the key of *excellence.* He asked, "What do the other car dealers offer by way of guarantee?" The answer was the stock, "12 months/12,000 miles." Garson Rice initiated the "three year/100,000 mile guarantee."

Next he believes in *Advertising.* "Doing business without advertising is like winking at your girl in the dark; you know what you're doing, but no one else does."

And finally, Rice says, "We are in the *people business.* We developed what we call a 'fanaticism about the customer'; you've got to keep them happy." Let me list those seven keys again:

Persistence
Expectation
Concentration
Enthusiasm
Excellence
Advertising
People-oriented

I can just hear the "Negative Nellies" of life saying, "That's crazy; it won't work." But articles are not written about "Negative Nellies." They are written about record holders like Garson Rice.

Are You a "Negative Nelly?"

The Trouble with stories like the one above is that we find them so easy to rationalize. "Garson who?" "Greensboro where?" Oh, that could never happen here! It could never happen to *me!*

I fly to speaking engagements around the country quite a lot. A few months ago I was on a plane and a little old lady sat next to the window in the seat behind me. Her husband sat next to her. She said in a voice louder than she realized, "I don't like riding on these planes. Folks get on these things with guns and knives" (that got everyone's attention). She said, "They take you places you don't want to go." (By now the pilot was leaning out of the cockpit looking at her, and the stewardess was alarmed.)

Well, the plane taxied to the end of the runway, and burst up through the clouds. It was a lovely day for flying. I didn't think of the little old lady again until our wheels hit the runway at the next airport. At that precise moment, her husband said in his little, squeaky voice, "You see honey, we made it all right." To which she bellowed, *"We ain't there yet!"*

I started to ask her if she was a member of the Church of Christ. I've met a lot of folks like that in my preaching, and I'll bet you've met a lot in your business. You know the sort: they can ruin anything you say. If you say, "Lovely day, isn't it?" they'll reply, "Well you know the saying, 'the calm before the storm.' " Or, "Things are really going good, aren't they?" and they'll reply, "So far."

You know the difference in a psychotic and a neurotic, don't you? The psychotic believes two plus two equals five, and if you talk to him long enough, he'll convince you it's true. The neurotic *knows* two and two is four . . . but it worries him!

Choose to Serve

The apostles of Jesus were holding a Muhammed Ali conference. Peter was saying "I'll be the greatest in the kingdom." John disagreed, "No, I'll be the greatest." Then the Lord walked up and said, "Now if you really want to be the greatest, be the servant of all" (Matt. 23:11).

I can just feel the rejection of that statement. I can hear the cynics saying, "No way! I'm not being anybody's doormat. I've got my rights. I'm not letting anybody walk on me. I'm looking out for old number One."

But, you know, Ramada Inn got to looking at that principle. And when I check in there, they follow it. They say, "Mr. Phillips, we're honored to have you with us. We'll carry your bags to your room. We'll clean the room, even the bathroom. Your room has a color TV and a telephone. We'll give you room service, transportation to the airport, rent you a car, make a room reservation in the next town. Is there anything else we can do for you?"

Now why do they do that? You say, "I guess they want to be a servant, doormat organization." No, man, *it's because they want your money!* And they get it too. They have thousands of happy customers, and make millions of dollars profit. That's why positive thinking speakers say, "You can get anything in life you want if you just help enough other people get what they want."

Now, some people can hear stories like this and still don't see it. They're sort of like the drunk walking down the street who saw a guy barbecuing a chicken in his back yard on a rotary spit. The drunk watched for a while and then exclaimed, "Buddy, it ain't never gonna work." The guy looked up from his work, "Why do you say that?" The drunk replied, "Your organ ain't playing and your monkey's on fire."

Old Bible Story: New Meaning

As a child, my Sunday school teacher told us about the Tower of Babel (Gen. 11:1–6). It went something like this. "Wicked people wanted to build a tower higher than anyone had ever built one before. God didn't want them to build it. So he confused their languages and scattered them over the face of the earth. That's how we got different languages and races in the world." The story was usually followed with the encouraging word, "Next Sunday we'll be in Genesis, chapter twelve, and we'll study about Abraham." It was years later when I caught the full meaning of the story.

That one verse (Gen. 11:6) contains probably the most exciting news for positive thinkers ever written. It says that "nothing will be withheld" from: (1) The people who learn to work with other people in unity; (2) The people with "singleness of purpose"; (3) The people who can dream and imagine big things; and (4) The people with a mind to apply hard work to get their project done.

A father enrolled his son in college. He said to the college president, "Isn't there an easier way? Isn't there a shortcut to all this expense and time?" And to his surprise the president said, "Oh, yes, there are lots of shortcuts. It all depends on what you want to make of your boy."

So I say to you, dear reader: Dream big dreams, dream right dreams, dedicate yourself to the hard work that success demands, and you will have all the prosperity you can handle!

CHAPTER FOUR

Developing the Power of Enthusiasm

It is said that the late Mr. Wrigley had a sign on the wall in his office which read, "Nothing Worthwhile Is Ever Accomplished Without Enthusiasm." I believe it! Enthusiasm is as powerful as dynamite and as contagious as the measles! Emerson said, "Every great and commanding movement in the world is the triumph of enthusiasm." Garson L. Rice recognized the power of enthusiasm (previous chapter) and it helped him set the world's record in Toyota sales.

A sales manager once said to his salesmen, "Men, if you show up for work and you've left your brains at home, we don't say much. But the day you get here without your enthusiasm, you're fired!"

But there's so much negativism in the world today that it is hard for the average man and woman to stay excited and enthused about life. It's not that there's nothing to be excited about, it's just that our attention is always on the negative! And if you don't watch it, the cynicism and impossibility thinkers will "rain on your parade," "water down your optimism," and "steal your dreams." Let a man lose everything but his enthusiasm, and he'll recover, but when he loses his enthusiasm, there just isn't anything to lift him to victory.

"Full of God"

Enthusiasm comes from two Greek words, "En Theos," meaning "God in you," or "full of God." So being enthusiastic is being the way God made you to be. The enthusiast is therefore "normal." It follows that if you're not enthusiastic, something is wrong, and you are not normal, like a person with a fever. Something needs to be set right, so that you can return to being your normal enthusiastic self.

You were born with enthusiasm. Did you ever watch a baby? My, how enthusiastic they are! They are excited, alive, vibrant and active! They want to see everything, do everything, and be a part of everything. Little children have no fear. It is not until adults plant these fears into them that they lose this normal vibrancy God has given them. Little children love the world. They believe everything is all right and is all for them. They believe they can do anything. They have no prejudices or fears until we teach them these negative things.

Is it any wonder, therefore, that Jesus said, "except you be converted and become as 'little children,' you cannot enter into the kingdom of heaven" (Matt. 18:3).

Huxley said, "The genius of the human being is to carry the spirit of the child into old age."

The Bible Urges Enthusiasm

The Bible says, "Whatever your hand finds to do, do it with all your might" (Ecc. 9:10). And again, "Whatever you do, work at it with all your heart, as working for the Lord, not for men" (Col. 3:23). We are urged to "Love the Lord your God with all your heart, and with all your soul, and with all your mind" (Matt. 22:37).

Anything that is worth doing is worth giving your all to. No one can get excited about mediocrity!

Christian Enthusiasm

To those of you who share my faith in Jesus Christ, the term, "negative Christian," is a contradiction. Christians are possessors of the famous four F's! They have (1) *Forgiveness.* Through their faith in Jesus, their repentance and their baptism, they enjoy forgiveness from every sin. They have a brand new start. This is why the early church "praised God and had favour with all the people" (Acts 2:47). They have (2) *a Father.* The best thing you can know about God is that he is your Father. Jesus taught us to pray, "Our Father, Who is in heaven." He is a Father who loves us and cares for our needs. We have (3) *Family.* Man, I wish we could get it on straight that church is "family." We take all those terms (i.e. "born again," "child of God," etc.) and make them "better felt than told," when all the time they are as basic as anything in life. We are all very familiar with these principles in physical life. We know we were born

into a family. We know what it means to have
parents, brothers, and sisters; and we know the
joy of "family reunion." Then we make these con-
cepts so "fuzzy" in religion. Hey, folks, church is
"family," where God's people are brothers and sisters and where worship is a "family reunion." God
is our "Father," and we ought to act like he is.
That makes church worship take on a whole new
meaning.

And we also have (4) *Future.* The rewards of
being a Christian are great now, and the "pension
plan" is out of sight. This is God's world. Heaven
is being prepared for us, and we are "Heirs of
God" (Rom. 8:17).

My Christian friends, this is precisely why we
sing such songs as "Blessed Assurance, Jesus is
Mine," "Amazing Grace," and "What a Fellowship."
Enthusiasm isn't an act. It is Christians caught
in the act of being "normal."

You've got to have enthusiasm to sell your product, to enrich your marriage, to bridge the generation gap between you and your kids. And how do
we develop this great power?

Think Enthusiastic!

Remember the chapter on "choice"? You can
choose to think enthusiastically or negatively! It's
really up to you! Henry David Thoreau said that
he would lie in bed each morning before getting
up and tell himself all the good news he could
think of. And there is always lots of good news.
"Grab the newspaper," as my good friend Cavett

Robert says, "and look in the obituary column. Find out that your name is missing! That's good news, isn't it? Now your biggest worry is how all those people managed to die in alphabetical order!"

We have a lot of negative garbage to overcome in order to think enthusiastically. The evening news is so negative that it will practically drive you out of your mind. Oh, and avoid soap operas! Those characters are always in trouble (all kinds of trouble), and as soon as they get out, another star is introduced who is, guess what . . . "in trouble." Life just isn't that bad! So think of all the good and keep that in your mind. The Bible puts it this way: "whatever things are true, noble, right, pure, lovely, admirable, excellent or praiseworthy . . . think about such things" (Phil. 4:8). Paul is reminding you of two things: (1) you have the power to think about what you choose to think about, and (2) there are always lots of good things to think about.

Be a "Joy Spreader"

Are you a "joy spreader" or a "doom and gloom spreader"? It starts off with the way you feel as you wake up in the morning! Do you say, "Good morning God," or is it "Good God . . . *morning*"? And don't be a fault finder! There's no prestige, pay, or power in fault finding. There are those people whose constant drabble is that this country is going to the dogs, the church is failing, youth is going down the drain, and nobody cares anymore! Hey, man, there's some of that to be sure, but it's sort of like the little jingle: "Two convicts looked through prison bars; one saw mud . . . the other, stars." What are you looking for? And where are you looking? You can see what you want to see! And since the good and bad are both there for your attention, why not spread the good and work to eliminate the bad?

Place the best connotation on everything and everybody. Give folks the benefit of the doubt. Expect the best from people and situations, and you'll get the best! We get about what we expect!

Give Your Best!

The world hates "goof-offs." We can tolerate and even cheer a losing team that has done it's best. We can cheer with the thousands of marathon runners in Boston each year who cross the finish line after more than a thousand have already crossed it ahead of them. But the world cannot abide a lazy, good-for-nothing who does not give his best. The crowd will boo a couple of boxers who lovingly dance together, arm in arm, and never throw a punch!

So what about your job? You say, well, it isn't much of a job. Then give it your best, and believe it into greatness. If you choose to work for a company, then give it your best or change companies. If you don't give your best, both you and the company lose.

Give your marriage your best. It's a crime how many men work to "make the sale" and then don't "service the account." Before you married you thought she was sweet enough to eat, and now you wish you had. Well, pitch in there. Spice up your marriage with a little romance, throw in some compliments, give a little thoughtfulness, and watch your marriage bloom into something exciting and alive! Enthusiasm does wonders for a marriage!

Apply these three principles of enthusiasm to your life and watch an exciting change come into your world!

CHAPTER FIVE

Winning over Worry

In this chapter, I'm going to touch on America's number one problem—worry! Worry sidetracks more people than probably any other thing. It is responsible for getting us off that "straight line" to our goals.

Isn't it amazing that worry should be such a problem in the world's richest country? We have more than half the world's wealth, while our population is only about 6% of the total world population.

Why should Americans worry when we have our free enterprise system, our democracy, and our freedoms? We may never know the reasons behind this strange phenomenon. Most of the world would gladly trade places with us, but we persist in worrying! Our yearly intake of tranquilizers would sink the largest navy!

In a survey at a leading American university, it was found that the chief problem among college students was worry, that they just didn't have what it takes—a feeling of inadequacy.

Worry! The Slow Killer

Man literally worries himself to death. Worry is a contributing cause in a hundred diseases. It is present in ulcers, sleepless nights, neuroses, depression, and defeatism. It no doubt contributes to tension, high blood pressure, and heart disease.

Worry does so much harm and absolutely no good at all. It cannot make black hair white, but it can make it fall out. It can harm every tissue in the body. "Nerves" is often just a worry problem.

Worry changes your appearance, wrinkles your brow, affects your speech, influences how you dress, chooses your colors for you, and alters your personality.

Worry About What?

You name it, and Americans will worry about it! It is estimated that 90% of the things we worry about never come to pass. If our teenagers are out, we worry that they might be involved in an accident, we worry that they might be introduced to drugs . . . they could be robbed . . . or worse yet, raped! On our jobs, we worry that we might be fired . . . that we won't get that raise . . . that we will be passed over, and someone else will get the promotion. We worry that we might go bankrupt!

We also worry about our health! As we get older, every twitch, every irregular beat of the heart and every pain becomes a potential terminal illness.

We worry if we think we have symptoms and if we have no symptoms. We worry about whether one of those terrible diseases will creep up unawares and strike without notice. After all, the man down the street was healthy as an ox . . . until the day the hearse came! I laughed with Paul Harvey as he said, "Never have those who like to worry had such a wide variety of subjects about which to worry."

Matthew 6:25–34

Jesus really went to work on the problem of worry while he was on earth. His followers were much the same as we are today. They worried that if they followed Jesus they would not be able to pay their bills, to clothe their families, or to meet tomorrow's obligations. Jesus' little sermon is certainly needed today. Look at it verse by verse.

He says, "Don't worry about life . . . life is more important than food . . . and the body is more important than clothes." He reminds us that God takes care of the birds. They do well because God set natural laws to care for them. And then Jesus chides us with, "aren't you much more valuable than they?" We are then told to look at the lilies of the field. And, oh my, aren't they beautiful around Easter! White, with green leaves, tall and beautiful like a bride ready for her wedding. The Lord says, "Solomon in all his glory was never as beautiful as these lilies." And then he adds,

"If God clothes the grass of the field, and the birds of the air, shall He not much more take care of you? O ye of little faith?"

He then makes a promise, and what a promise it is! If we will just get our priorities straight—Jesus calls it "seek first the kingdom of God" and "all these things will be given you as well."

Now come on down to earth, and let's ask, "Can we really count on this promise?" Will God really lead us to opportunity, help us with our jobs, and provide us with the necessities of life? The answer comes ringing back, "Try me, and see if I won't throw open the windows of heaven and pour out so much blessing that you will not have room enough for it" (Mal. 3:10). Now, neighbor, what was it you were worrying about?

Don't Just Stand There . . . Do Something!

Let's get practical about handling this problem of worry! We have already suggested that we "think on the right things." Now we're going to add, *"Don't guess bad outcomes."* The real difference in positive thinking and negative thinking is in "possible outcomes." The positive thinker, seeing the possibility of success, gears his thinking to that end, adjusts his efforts, and confidently moves in that direction. Success comes as he expected, and he enjoys it.

The negative thinker, on the other hand, sees the possibility of failure and locks in on that possibility. He unwittingly helps bring it to pass.

Let me give you a painful illustration. I was more of a worrywart, a negative thinker, in high school. One year on our baseball team, they played me in right field where I couldn't mess up too much. One year I played "floater" (between second base and center field). All season, I think only one ball came out there, and I worried that I might miss it (I did). I would step up to the plate to take my turn at bat and say, loud enough for the others to hear, "Here goes another out"—and I always struck out, grounded out, or flied out! The coach asked me, "Why do you bother batting? You have already decided the outcome before you put the bat in your hand." And you know, that was the truth. But I was afraid! I worried that I would make a mess, that I would let the team down, that I would be humiliated. Well I got to thinking about that before the next season. I decided the very best home run hitter strikes out now and then. It's no big deal. Well obviously, I didn't become a major league player, but I'll guarantee that my batting average went up the next year, and I had a lot more fun. And more importantly, I wasn't worried anymore, and my self-image went up a few more notches.

The Masks We Wear

I suppose we all have an assortment of masks that we wear. We wear them because we are terrified that if the special people in our lives knew what we were really like, they would reject us.

Friendship and love means that we take off a few more masks around these special people. But we never take off that last one. The reason? If we take it off and are rejected, there is nothing left. We just don't think we can stand that.

Again, God comes to our rescue. It used to terrify me that God "knew it all." I'd hear preachers say, "God knows all about you," and it would scare the daylights out of me. And then one day I discovered that God is the only one who has seen behind all the masks and, having done so, still declares his love for us and wants us saved and in his family. Boy, oh boy, that's just great! No more worry! I can just be myself around the Lord. I can ask him about my hangups, discuss my flaws, seek his help, and nothing can make him quit loving me (Rom. 8:35–39).

Correctly Assess Yourself!

Some of us find it impossible to accept a compliment! This has its roots in our self-esteem and fosters more worry in our lives. Someone says to you, "You look nice tonight," and you reply, "Oh, not really . . . this old rag?"

Come on now, you stood in front of that mirror for half an hour getting your own final inspection. When you thought you looked great, you went out to meet the world only to reject every compliment the world tried to give. Look friend, what you are is enough! Remember the lesson again: God created you, and "He didn't make no junk"!

Correctly Assess God!

Not only accept yourself as you are, but understand that God can use you to do great things. In fact, he may have a great plan in store for your life. Hey, God can write as well with a 19¢ ball point pen as he can with a $50.00 gold one! I'm sure that's why Paul could say, "I can do all things through Christ" (Phil. 4:13).

Sin At the Root!

Finally, I fear that sin is at the root of the worry problem! We live in God's world, but many don't want to live his way! So we reject his will, do our own thing; and a worry-strained, fear-filled, anxiety-twisted life is the result. Friend, you have been designed by the Designer, and he has a purpose for your life. You can fit into his will as water fits into the shape of whatever it is poured into. Let him fill your life with forgiveness and fruitfulness as well as success and happiness.

A little boy had trouble memorizing the 23rd Psalm. Try as he would, he just couldn't get it right. Finally, one day in his Sunday School class he made his most valiant try. "The Lord is my Shepherd," he said, and then his mind would go blank. Finally in desperation he said, "The Lord is my Shepherd . . . why should I worry." I think he finally got it right!

CHAPTER SIX

Motivation: The Key to Success

The dictionary defines *motivation* as "the thing that makes one feel, move or act." The Bible urges us to "stimulate to wholesome thinking" (2 Pet. 3:1); "spur one another on . . . encourage one another" (Heb. 10:24,25). And it is obvious that we all need motivating if we are to dream big dreams and reach them.

Do you remember the fellow being chased by a bear? In the open field he passed only one tree, and the lowest branch was a good fifteen feet off the ground. The bear was getting closer, so in desperation he leaped for the limb. He missed—but he caught it on the way down! Now that's motivation. It helps us reach heights we otherwise could not reach.

Motivation: Part of Our Everyday Lives

We are motivated by various things to go to work, to go to school, to dress neatly, to make plans and carry them out, to buy, sell, etc. We are motivated by money, by the desire for an education, by the thrill of excitement, by profit, fear, love, and many other things.

When you see a sloppy, lazy, spineless, fat, dirty, quitter, he's just not motivated. If you can motivate him, you will change his life. But so many are like the sailor on the park bench. He said, "Honey, if I was just an octopus, I'd wrap all those tentacles around you and give you a squeeze you'd never forget." But she replied, "Come on, sailor, you're not using the talent you've got." Some people just aren't motivated!

Motivation can help you have a more positive attitude. It can help you get a different job, a better job, and a higher paying job. Motivation can enrich your marriage and bring you closer to your children.

Motivation applied spiritually can make worship more enjoyable and effective. It can result in a growing, outreaching church.

Motivated by Fear and Love

Fear is a legitimate motivation, but it won't last. Let me illustrate. When the first folks became Christians (Acts 2:37ff), their motivation was fear. They had killed Jesus, and the preacher was convicting them of this crime. They cried out in fear, "What shall we do?" They were told good news: If they would just repent and be baptized, they would be forgiven of all sins. It is stated, "they gladly received this word," and 3,000 were baptized on that day.

But fear as a motivation won't last. You just

can't keep on running scared. Fear must give way to love. As he contemplated the love of God, the apostle Paul said, "the love of Christ leaves me no choice." He felt completely drawn by this love.

David and Goliath

One of the most thrilling stories in the Bible is in 1 Samuel chapter 17. It is the story of little David and how he killed the giant, Goliath. David was too young for the army, but his father sent him to the valley of Elah where his brothers were fighting the Philistines. David was bringing food and supplies from home. While there, he heard the nine-and-a-half-foot Goliath make his challenge: "Send me any Israelite to do battle. Whoever wins, the opposing army will become their slaves." It was a clear challenge. There were no takers.

Little David saw the situation entirely different than his older, soldier brothers. Motivated by his belief in God, he saw the giant as "defying the army of the living God." David went to fight Goliath, armed only with a small sling and five smooth stones from the brook. The heavily armored giant cried out in disgust and defiance at this mere lad coming to fight against him. But David's answer was, "You come against me with sword and spear; I come against you in the name of the Lord Almighty." You see, comparison is all relative. The army of Israel compared the giant to their size; David compared him to God. The difference was enough for the victory.

Applied to us, what I'm saying is that if you

believe in an Almighty God who created the universe, made you in his image, and rules the world, you should feel confident that he can help with that job you need, that $150 car payment coming due next week, or any other problem that comes your way.

Two Kinds of Motivation

The first kind of motivation is the kind that comes to you. Doesn't it make you feel good to get an unsolicited compliment or to hear some really good news? Doesn't that motivate you and excite you? And it's especially good if it comes at the beginning of the day, for then you can savor it all day long. It really "makes your day."

Now if that news or that phone call happens to be "bad," it can "ruin your whole day." The trouble with this is that you can't depend on getting this good motivation every day, at the beginning of each day. So you've got to do the next best thing. You've got to start out your own day with good news. There are several ways of doing this. You can adopt Thoreau's method of lying in bed and telling yourself all the good news you can think of; or you can give someone else compliments and let it rub off on yourself.

Or you can begin the day listening to the right kind of cassette tapes. I recommend Zig Ziglar's "How to Stay Motivated," and of course I recommend my own albums for this use.

I have made a brilliant discovery. I found that I don't shave with my ears. So while I'm shaving, my ears are free to listen to positive-thinking, motivational tapes. Carefully select what you listen to, and listen to them over and over again. About the seventh time you hear them, your mind actually begins to think in a positive manner. And this motivator will become a way of life to you.

So you can take what motivation comes, or you can make it happen through cassettes, books, and attending Positive Thinking Rallies. Either way, it's a great way of life.

Practical Pointers on Motivation

Choose to be motivated! How do you really want to feel? What do you really want to do, to have? Go after it! Every day, do something to move yourself closer to your goal! No one can destroy your motivation without your consent!

Absorb motivational things! Choose what you read, hear, and see! Stay away from the bad, read the good regularly and repetitively (spaced repetition). Fill your mind again and again with good things, and you'll have no trouble at all thinking positively. Positive thinkers *do* get positive results!

Stay around the right people and things! The Bible says, "Bad company corrupts good morals" (1 Cor. 15:33). Alcoholics must not hang around bars if they want to quit drinking. You can't hang around with pessimists and negative people and be a positive thinker. Stay away from events that drain off your optimism!

Pray! Tell God what you want to do and want

to be! Ask him specifically to make you more excited with life, more motivated to do right, more cheerful in all you do.

Remember, you've got what it takes to handle anything life throws at you. Motivation is the key to get you going in the right direction!

CHAPTER SEVEN

Recharging through Relaxation

"A relaxed attitude lengthens a man's life" (Prov. 14:30). If we could only relax and lose our tensions, we could capture that powerful strength the Lord has given us all. Then we could get about the business of setting and reaching great goals.

Tension: A National Problem

According to an article in a recent national magazine, there are thirty million Americans with a drug abuse problem, and about two thirds of them are women! There are over 1500 brand-name drugs. In a single year, over 229,000,000 prescriptions were filled for mood-altering drugs. Eighty per cent of the prescriptions for amphetamines were for women, and two thirds of all drugs are prescribed for women. There are over 10 million alcoholics in America and half of them are women.

It may sound like I am really coming down strong on women, but these are alarming statistics. They point out that we have too much tension and stress in our lives, and this problem is seen especially in women. A few years ago the statistics were heavily slanted toward men. Something is causing this alarming increase in the problem of tension among women and the use of drugs is related to the problem.

Women Speak to the Problem

The article mentioned above went on to probe for answers to the drug abuse problem among America's women, and this is what they were told: "increased stress in the American way of life, tension caused by her husband's job versus her own, inflation, childbirth, childrens' problems, absence of purpose, alienation, and the 'hard sell' by the drug industry on commercials to get women to believe that the answer to all their problems lies inside a capsule."

Humans have become uptight. We are living too fast, too tense, and we've lost the art of relaxation.

There Is Strength in Relaxation!

Have you ever watched athletes exercising before competition? All that jumping around, jogging in place, and exercises are called "loosening up." An athlete knows that the edge can be taken off his preparation if he is too tense. Strength and power come from his ability to relax and hang loose. Many a race has been lost because an athlete tensed up, pulled a muscle and had to pull out of the competition.

It happens that way in life. All of us have problems to cope with. There are challenges that demand our best. A lot is at stake (perhaps a promotion). We want to do our best, so we psyche ourselves up and out, and absolutely go "bananas." Our bodies feel exhausted, our minds refuse to think straight, and we end up doing the poorest job we ever did. Isn't there a way to avoid these setbacks and even more, a way to sharpen our minds and bodies to do their best at our bidding? Fortunately, there is.

Observe Babies!

Babies have so much energy, yet they are so relaxed. They are dynamos of excitement, yet they can go to sleep at the drop of a hat. Why is this? It is simply because they are relaxed. Because they are so relaxed, they have unlimited strength and energy at their disposal. They are strangely paradoxical in that they can give all they've got in activity, and then they can sleep through anything.

Now here's the answer. Babies are created by a loving God who made them completely relaxed. They will stay that way until grownups teach them all the fears, problems, and hangups that cause us to be uptight. You see, tension is "man-learned." We did not get it from God. The more we become like "little children" (Matt. 18:3), the more we become as relaxed as God made us.

You see, as we grew up, we lost this God-given quality and allowed impure thoughts to enter our minds (hatred, jealousy, sinfulness, etc.). When relaxation goes, serenity goes with it, and uptightness takes its place. Our need is to return to "childlikeness," not "childishness"!

Thank God that he, the Creator, is also the *recreator!* At any age or any stage, we can reverse the process, shed our tensions, relearn the art of relaxation, and recover the power God wants us to have.

Relaxation Is a Learned Art!

I remember a particularly good "Bus Seminar" held at our church a couple of years ago. Folks had come from many states to learn how to use buses to reach people in their areas. I think we did a lot of good, but it was exhausting, and when it was over I felt really "beat." I said to my wife, "Let's get in the car and drive."

Presently we came to a park. I told my wife, "Honey, sit where you want to sit, I've got to walk a bit." I came upon a babbling brook and sat down beside it. I began to stare into the bubbling water. It was a lovely summer day, and I was in the shade of the big trees next to the brook. After about half an hour I noticed, to my delight, that my tensions were entirely gone. I was refreshed and the energy had returned to my body. My mind felt alert and ready to go. And it had only taken 30 minutes.

Excitedly, I found my wife and exclaimed to her, "We've got to get us a creek." I really meant it! At that time we lived in a crowded suburban neighborhood. I saw what this "communing with nature" had done to my mind and body. Instantly it became

more important than anything to get where I could
walk by the creek at will, listen to the birds sing,
and watch that lovely babbling water.
We began our search for a new place to live.
While you dream, I encourage you to "go all the
way." Don't close your mind to anything. If for
some reason you can't make it all happen, then
get the next best thing. In our case, we wanted
space, trees, a creek, and a two-story house.
Through the providence of God (I feel) we got it
all. We found a lovely, wooded housing area just
out of the city. Highways connected it with my
work so I could get there in minutes. It had it
all! It had trees—hundreds of them, including four
huge pecan trees, just right for building that lovely
two-story house right in the middle of—and a wan-
dering creek running right through the property.
We planned the breakfast nook where it would
capture this scenic beauty. The upstairs bedroom
is large, including a fireplace and a balcony that
leads right out into one of those large pecan trees.
It has a view of the creek and wooded area, and
is worth its weight in gold in relaxation. It is designed for walking, meditating, thinking, and un-
winding.

Dear friend, I described this at length to show
that you can learn the art of relaxation. If you
don't handle your tensions, they will "handle you."

Now, if such a step as ours seems too great for
you, then pick a place you can visit often. The psalm-
ist David must have often walked with nature.
His psalms (especially the 23rd) show it! "He mak-
eth me to lie down in green pastures; He leadeth
me beside the still waters. He restoreth my soul."

Oh, my! Try finding such a place. Lie on your back in the grass, look off into a blue sky, and repeat the words of the 23rd psalm. Just try to remain tense while doing this. I don't think it is possible.

Keep a Supply of "Mental Relaxation Pictures"

I go with a group to the Bible Lands every other year. One of my treasured activities while in Jerusalem is to wake up at 4:00 A.M. and take a taxi up to the Mt. of Olives (from where Jesus ascended back to heaven). I take all who want to come and we watch the sunrise over Bethany (home of Mary, Martha, and Lazarus—Jesus' close friends). Then we walk down the hill into the Garden of Gethsemane where Jesus often went to pray with his disciples. In the peace of that olive grove, we fan out among the trees just to think and pray. Someone will invariably begin the song:

I come to the garden alone,
While the dew is still on the roses,
And the voice I hear, falling on my ear,
The Son of God discloses.
And He walks with me, and He talks with me,
And He tells me I am His own,
And the joy we share, as we tarry there,
None other, has ever known.

The sun is to our backs. Our faces are toward the old walled city of Jerusalem. We can almost see Jesus praying for that city,

*Oh, Jerusalem, Jerusalem, Thou that killest
the prophets and stonest them that are sent
to thee. How often would I have gathered thy
children together, as a hen gathereth her chickens under her wings, and ye would not* (Matt.
23:37).

Even now, I can close my eyes, and see that
scene vividly before me. This means that I can
mentally revisit that mountain and that garden
at any time I want! And every time I do, my body
and mind relax, and my spirit is recharged for
the challenges of the day.

My reading friend, you have memories like this.
Remember a night on a cruising ship, with the
moon making its silvery ribbon across the waves.
The wind beats its gentle breeze against your face,
and you feel that all is right with the world.

Search your memory for priceless gems such
as these. They are there, locked in your subcon-
scious mind. Take them out at will. And in any
given five minute span, you can draw them out,
relive their delicious pleasure, and relax your mind
and replenish your strength.

Is there a pressured committee meeting coming
up in ten minutes? Good. Close and lock your door
and take a five minute, mind-relaxing visit to your
"memory spot."

Are you burdened with pains and problems
brought on by our jet-age living? Take out one of
your mental pictures and relive it with absorbed
enjoyment! You'll find that your body has returned
to its normal relaxed state, and your mind has

sharpened to meet your problems with workable solutions. And best of all, no one can rob you of that pleasurable filing system. Use it whenever you need it.

I've done enough writing for now. And you've done enough reading. Let's sneak off for a five-minute, instant replay of one of these relaxing enjoyable, mind pictures. See you later!

CHAPTER EIGHT

The Flesh Is Willing,
It's the Spirit That's Weak

"The spirit is willing, but the flesh is weak." That's a Bible verse, but it is also a "cop out" used by those who want to explain away their failure to produce and accomplish. In most cases, the opposite is the truth, as I've entitled this chapter. But first, let's look at the Bible story from which the verse is taken.

It was the end of Jesus' ministry. He was soon to be crucified. It was to be a long night. The disciples had been with him all day and into the night. They had walked from the upper room to the crest of Mt. Olive then down into the Garden of Gethsemane. There Jesus took Peter, James, and John with him for more earnest prayer. Jesus knew the end was near, and he agonized in prayer. The Bible says that great drops of sweat (like blood) fell from his brow. He asked his three friends to stay for a moment while he went on alone, a little further into the garden, and prayed. He prayed a long time. When he returned, he found his disciples sleeping. It was not a stern rebuke, but with understanding he said, "The spirit is willing, but the flesh is weak." It is actually more of a compliment. These disciples loved Jesus. They would soon die for him. But their bodies could not keep up with the longing of their spirits.

The Flesh Is Willing!

In many cases the opposite is true! We use this statement as an excuse for not doing, accomplishing, and growing. We wake up on a cold morning faced with the necessity of getting our bodies out of bed, and getting to work. We say, "the spirit is willing, but the flesh is weak." Church members say the same about their absence from worship services, "the spirit is willing, but the flesh is weak."

But the truth is "The flesh is willing." It is the spirit that is weak.

Our bodies are capable of astounding feats. Witness the astronauts. See our young people go on "wilderness trips" where they climb mountains and endure great stress factors. See housewives who tackle and complete the Boston marathon (26.2 miles). In fact, among the finishers of the Boston marathon two years ago was a one-legged man and two blind men. Set world records, they did not, but they entered . . . and they finished. I repeat, our flesh is capable of great things. We don't have a flesh problem! The problem is with the spirit, which is another way of saying "attitude."

The flesh is not only willing but is anxiously waiting to be put into action. It is filled with all the things the spirit lacks. It has grit, pluck, and nerve! It can withstand, if we only put it to the test. America was carved out of the wilderness by men who laid bodies on the line against all odds and came out victorious. They did so without welfare, food stamps, social security, or medicare! Then we stepped in, insured against failure, and killed incentive.

Walt Stack

Being a runner, I take "Runners' World" magazine. In every issue there is Walt Stack advertising some watch that can endure all he puts it through in his daily workouts. He is over 70 and began running at age 58. His daily routine includes bicycling 10 miles, running 17 miles across the Golden Gate Bridge and back, swimming for 30 minutes in the cold water of San Francisco bay and then thawing out in a 200 degree sauna.

I say, "Do you think you can do that?" and you reply, "Man, I don't even *want* to do that," and that's just the point! You *could* if you *wanted* to! My point, in case you're missing it, is that the *flesh is willing!* You may not want to be a Walt Stack. But whatever you want to be, your body can handle!

What is missing is that spiritual energy called "enthusiasm." When we are enthusiastic, we take on the characteristics that go with it. That energy brings action and that action brings brightness of attitude, which culminates in goal-setting and goal-reaching.

Must Be a Bit of a Fanatic!

I'm constantly amazed at folks who are really enthusiastic about a particular sports team. They go to every game, at home or away. They'll sit in the stands in a sub-zero blizzard to cheer their team to victory. They are commonly known as "fans." If a person does the same thing about church, he is called a "fanatic."

But to be successful at anything, you must have a passion for doing it. If you would move someone else to action, you must be moved to action yourself. Public speakers do this. They pace up and down, psyching themselves up before addressing an audience. They have to get their adrenalin flowing and their excitement to fever pitch, then they can generate that same excitement in their audience. Salesmen do the same thing. You can sell what you're sold on. You can overcome fear, pain, and timidity in this way. Spirit offers more than excitement, motivation, and incentive. Behind spirit (enthusiasm) lies inspiration, behind inspiration lies passion, and behind passion lies will! These (like stairs) provide the drive and determination to get us where we want to go. They are what finally separates us from the rest of the pack.

We Get What We Are Obsessed With!

Alan Shepherd was America's first sub-orbital astronaut! He wanted to go to the moon, but a health problem got him grounded and stuck with a desk job. But still, he vividly dreamed of going to the moon. It was sheer determination (spirit), more than anything else, that finally made that dream into reality. Tears flowed both on the moon and on earth when Alan Shepherd finally landed and beamed back to earth, "It was a long trip, but I finally made it."

We Are Divided Into Three Classes!

What then does the Bible verse mean by, "the spirit is willing; the flesh is weak?"

1. "The flesh is willing, it's the spirit that's weak." This is where most of us live. We could if only we would; but lacking motivation and determination, we live our lives in mediocrity!

2. "Flesh and spirit working together." Like a team of fine horses, each asks and demands more of the other. It is beautiful to watch a man who has the spirit of determination. He demands much from his body, and in turn his body demands that his mind thinks higher and plans bigger, so it can do more.

3. "Spirit willing, flesh weak." This is where those disciples of Jesus were. Their spirits were so in tune to Jesus that their bodies literally could not keep up. This is a height that few people ever attain: the victory of spirit over body, minds so

sharp and active that it is not possible for their bodies to keep up. They are so attuned to God that they can never do all the things their spirits hunger to do.

Conclusion

Let's recognize the amazing capacity of our physical bodies and understand that we can go as high as we can dream. Now what are you waiting for? There are exciting goals to meet, and you've got what it takes. Get going!

CHAPTER NINE

Is This Train Going Anywhere?

Two men boarded a train and congratulated themselves that they were the only ones on that coach. They could get the choice seats and not have to be bothered by the usual crowded conditions. Pretty soon, the conductor came by and said, "You gentlemen will have to move to another car. You can't ride in here." They looked at each other knowingly. "No way," they replied, "We were the first ones on here. We have the choice seats, and we're not moving into any crowded car just so you won't have to walk through here." The conductor replied, "Suit yourselves! But this coach ain't going nowhere, 'cause it ain't hooked to nothin'."

I am sure that many of our lives are like that. We dress nicely, drive good cars, and engage in busy activity, but "we ain't goin' nowhere, 'cause we ain't hooked to nuthin'."

Just How Important Is It to Have Goals?

I fly a lot! Suppose I asked our pilot, "Where are we going today?" Suppose he said, "I don't know. It's a beautiful day. I thought we'd just fly around a little. We might land here and there, depending on how the mood strikes." Now, brothers and sisters, I've got better things to do than waste my time in that way.

I recently flew from Tulsa to Los Angeles. This meant I had to get to the Tulsa airport (a definite place) at a definite time. We flew to Los Angeles and landed at a definite time. Friends were there to pick me up and take me to a particular motel, and I spoke to several thousand at the Anaheim convention center that night. When you think about it, there were a lot of "definites" connected with that trip. With indefinite goals in mind, I surely would never have gotten there, my friends wouldn't have known when and where to meet me, and I wouldn't have had the joy of addressing that fine audience.

Many things hinge on definite goals! You can't take "just any road" and get there "sometime" in life. You can't just go to "any college," and major in "just anything" and end up being a successful doctor, lawyer, or engineer. It takes forethought, decision making, setting of definite goals, and taking the steps necessary to get there.

Rivers Flow in One Direction!

While we're talking about flying, I love to watch the ground when I fly, especially when I'm in a private airplane. (Jets fly too high for that.) There are few things that are more lovely than rivers seen from the air. Their silver stream ribbons its way, meandering lazily in one direction and then

another. But rivers are going in only one direction
. . . *down!* And brother, your life, without goals,
will go in only one direction . . . *down!*
And don't confuse activity with accomplishment!
Our lives are busy all right. We go at "break-neck"
speed, yet seem to accomplish almost nothing.
Even in churches, I see committees with their
meetings, activities, and busy-ness, and I see
church members with their tongues hanging out
from exhaustion. They are burdened and bombed
out, dashing and darting here and there. They
are at the point of collapse, yet they are accomplishing virtually nothing. And it is all because
they do not take the time to set clear objectives,
to pinpoint the goals they want to achieve, and
then do the things that get them there.

Single-mindedness

Remember that verse in Gen. 11:6? The people
had "one language." That doesn't mean Aramaic,
Hebrew, or even English. Lots of people speak
the same language but have no clear-cut goal.
What the verse really means is that they had singleness of purpose. They really wanted that tower.
They talked about it, they planned it, they dreamed
about it in their sleep. When the "Negative Nellies"
came on the scene with all the reasons it couldn't
be done, (i.e. "cost too much," "take too many work-
ers," "take too many years") they simply replied,
"we want that tower." It takes a dogged determination to accomplish a clearly-defined goal. A big
shot is just a little shot that keeps shooting.
The apostle Paul said, "One thing I do; forgetting

what is behind and straining toward what is ahead, I press on toward the goal to win the prize for which God has called me heavenward in Christ Jesus" (Phil. 3:13–14).

You must decide where you want to go in life, and then travel the road that leads there. It is as simple as that!

Ask Some Questions

Regardless of what goals we're talking about (life, job, marriage, spiritual), ask these soul-searching questions:

1. Where am I right now?
2. Where have I been?
3. Where do I really want to go?
4. What steps are necessary to get there?
5. Now *take the steps!*

Break the Bonds of Conformity

We blindly follow those who went before us. We accomplish what they did and what they told us we could do. We never thought about going beyond their horizons. As one sheep will blindly follow another to the slaughter, we follow one another in mediocrity. We accept imaginary ceilings, limits, fears, and obstacles. Why *can't* it be done? Why must we copy one another's failures just to prove we're loyal? Let's knock the 't' out of Can't and get going on some really big, exciting goals. You *Can!* You know you can!

CHAPTER TEN

Believe Your Life into Greatness

"Everything is possible for him who believes" (Mark 9:23).

You've heard it said, "What the mind of man can conceive and believe it can achieve." Well, it's so! "Two convicts looked through prison bars; one saw mud, the other, stars." Why do people who are raised in the same environment come out different? Why do some succeed while others fail, yet their abilities and opportunities seem equal? The key is *belief*.

Believers accomplish! The Wright brothers were believers. Can you imagine the ridicule they received as they built that first airplane? "You'll never get that thing off the ground, Orville." "That's the most ridiculous thing I've ever seen, Wilber." And now, all of a sudden . . . whoosh . . . there goes another 747!

Thomas A. Edison is a classic example of a believer. In his work to find a filament that would hold an electrical current, he had to try thousands of different things. One fellow said, "Mr. Edison, I don't see how you keep on. I understand you've had 3,000 failures." To which Edison hotly replied, "I've never had a failure in my life. I've just learned 3,000 ways it won't work. I'm getting closer all the time." And he did too. After nearly 10,000 experiments, he perfected the forerunner of the filament that keeps us all in light today. He was a believer.

Well, you say, believe in what?

Believe in Almighty God!

This country was founded by men and women of great faith in God. This faith was written into our constitution; it showed up in the Bill of Rights; it was even stamped on our coins. Our country is great today primarily because of its faith in God.

Let me illustrate the importance of this. I returned to my motel room one night after a speaking engagement. I don't usually watch much television, but this night I was tired and wanted something to just fill my mind and help me unwind. I turned on the TV and sat down on the edge of the bed to take off my coat and shoes. The TV didn't come on. I figured it was one of those old jobs that take a long time to warm up. So I took off the other shoe and then my tie and shirt. The TV still didn't come on. By then I was upset. "This must be the only motel room in this city with a TV that won't work. I don't watch much TV, and the only night I want to watch a little, the thing won't work." Well I did the only technical thing I knew to do . . . I kicked it. But it still didn't come on. By now I was so upset I thought of calling the manager and having him send a repairman over to fix the thing right then. But before I did that, I thought I'd check one more thing. I looked down, and sure enough, there was the cord lying on the floor. The set was unplugged!

It was some time later that I caught the real lesson in this. There was that TV with all its component parts: the genius of our age. Everything was in good working order, but until it was plugged in you couldn't even get a test pattern on it. It was six inches from the power source. Once plugged in, it worked beautifully.

Man is much the same. We have what it takes. God has designed us for success and greatness. But until we are hooked up to the Power, we are about as helpless as that TV. I think belief in God is important.

Believe In Your Country

People say all kinds of things about America. That's one of the beautiful things about our great country. We have the freedom to say what we please, even if it is bad. In many countries, you would be executed for saying some of the things Americans say about their own land.

Now I'm sure the people to whom I speak and those who read this book hold many and varied political views. But there is one thing I think I can safely say without contradiction; "George Bush is the greatest president we've got!"

You say, "Well George Bush is the only president

we've got." Okay, that's true, so let's try another statement. "America is the greatest country in the world." You can compare America to any country on earth. Nowhere else do people enjoy the freedoms and opportunities we enjoy in America. It's sort of like the fellow who was asked, "How's your wife?" He replied, "Compared to what?"

It's wonderful isn't it, how they built that Berlin Wall to keep us out! America has to have an "immigration quota" because so many want to be where you live. But I'm sure you've noticed we have no "Out-igration Quota"! Americans are free to leave anytime they think they've found something better!

Our marvelous free enterprise system gives such unlimited opportunities. Any American, with even a touch of Positive Attitude, can study American needs (even American "wants") and then busy himself supplying those needs—honestly, cheerfully, and dependably—and he'll have more than enough success in life.

Is Inflation a Problem?

Now I'll grant you we're all concerned with the high cost of living, but this, too, is relative. For example, I bought a house in 1955. It was a little frame, two-bedroom thing, without central air and heat. It cost me three years' salary. Now my wife and I live in our dream home, which is much larger than the original one and has many more luxuries. Yet it cost me only two and a half year's salary.

I bought my first new car in 1956. It was a

six-cylinder car, with no luxuries. It cost me six months' pay. Last July, my wife and I celebrated our silver anniversary, so I bought her a new silver car. It was much nicer than the '56 model and had so many more luxuries. It cost me three months' pay!

Suits have gone down a days pay (from 2 ½ to 1 ½), and (are you ready for this?) gasoline is also down from twenty years ago. It used to cost me 6 ½ minutes of work to buy a gallon of gas; it now costs me 4 ½ minutes per gallon.

I don't know about you, but I've got more of this world's goods than I've ever had before, and I figure I've got a choice. I can revert to the way I used to live twenty years ago, without all the luxuries of today, or I can continue to live the way I live today (the way I choose to live) and quit griping about it. And brother, that's my choice!

Believe in Your Fellow Man

Many of us are like the Charlie Brown character who said, "I believe in humanity; it's people I can't stand." Our problem is that the media has bombarded us with "man's inhumanity to man"; the Kinsey report has exposed man at his worst. It has made cynics of us all. We have become like the fellow in the hospital who was told he was dying. With his doctor on one side of the bed and his lawyer on the other, he exclaimed, "Well at least I'm going like Jesus; dying between two thieves."

There's a sign outside Milford, Texas, that pretty

well describes our fellowmen. It says, "Milford, Texas, city of 750 friendly people . . . and 3 or 4 old grouches." That's my nation; that's the church where I preach. Filled with absolutely great people . . . and 3 or 4 grouches.

The Garnett Road church runs 33 buses that bring in about 800 kids on a given Sunday. This activity puts us right out where the people are. On Sunday night I thought I'd do something different to show the people what we were doing and convince them of the value of people. I moved the pulpit, hooked on a lapel mike, got a little girl, and held her in my arms. "What's your name?" I asked. "Crissy!" "How old are you, Crissy?" And she held up two fingers. Then I proceeded to tell the audience that in 10 years, Crissy would be 12, and in another 10 she would be 22. "And what she becomes is largely up to us," I concluded with confidence. That went well, so I looked around for someone else. I should have quit while I was ahead.

"Come up here, Tommy," I said, as I spotted a 10-year-old boy. He was sitting there on the front row. He makes a habit of sitting by me most every Sunday. I got him up before the people and said, "Tommy, what are you going to be when you grow up?" "A preacher," he replied. Oh, I had a good one. So I asked "Why?" And Tommy said, "To tell people about Jesus and win souls to Christ." Oh, this was good. Then I made the mistake of asking, "Do you think you'll be better than me?" "I sure *hope* so," came his answer, and the house came down! And my spirits went up. What a thrill it would be if Tommy and a thousand other Tommy's in our congregation became "better than me" at winning souls for Jesus.

Yes, neighbor, you can believe in people. You can do business with people and win. Just follow the law of sowing and reaping found in Galatians 6:7: "Whatever a man sows, that shall he also reap."

There are three things about sowing and reaping that you need to keep in mind. You reap *what* you sow; you reap *more* than you sow; and you reap *later* than you sow! Follow this principle on your job, in your marriage, and in your church. Sow the right stuff, and success is yours.

Believe in Yourself!

Never forget that verse in Genesis (1:26) that says that you've been made in God's image. You are loveable and capable! If you believe you can, you will; if you believe you can't . . . you won't!

And the "what-if's" and "if only's" won't get it either! A fellow said to Joe Louis, former heavyweight champion of the world, "If I was as big as you, I'd go out into the woods and find the biggest bear I could find, and whip him with my bare hands." Mr. Louis replied, "There are bears in the woods your size!"

Am I getting through to you? I'm saying that you can believe in God, believe in your country, believe in your fellow-man, and believe in yourself, and you can overcome any obstacle and accomplish any goal.

The great Milton overcame his blindness, Beethoven overcame his deafness, Franklin Delano Roosevelt overcame his polio to become president of the United States, Lincoln did the same with his poverty, and Ulysses S. Grant his alcoholism. John Bunyan wrote Pilgrim's Progress in prison, and Benjamin Franklin was a 10-year-old, school dropout!

> *I had the blues, because I had no shoes,*
> *Until one day upon the street, I met a man*
>   *who had no feet.*

Believe, dear friend, and you are on your way to greatness!

CHAPTER ELEVEN

Keep Physically and Spiritually Fit

It was a lovely Summer day in June, 1970. I had just begun my ministry in Tulsa. And to enjoy this glorious time of year, a bunch of us were out playing flag football. Suddenly one of our ladies came running out on the field screaming for me to come quickly.

Our song leader was only 32 years old. It was hard to believe when she told us that he had had a heart attack, and he was already dead!

How can it be? And I still don't know the answer today! But one thing I know, I preach lots of unnecessary funerals for men (more than women) who should be in their prime. They should be reaching some of their earlier goals and really beginning to enjoy life. Yet they are struck down by heart attacks, strokes, and such like.

His doctor later told me, "Marvin, doctors figure that if they can get a patient through his forties, he has a pretty good chance of living a normal life." Through his forties? What in the world are we doing? What's happening to us? Or worse still, what are we neglecting that cuts us down when we are on the verge of really learning how to live and attaining the goals we dreamed?

And why, in this enlightened age, when we transplant hearts and kidneys, when we perform brain surgery . . . why have people failed to learn the simple rules of "preventive maintenance" that can enhance life, channel our powers, and give us zest as we approach achievement?

Wake Up, America!

Like the early morning TV show suggests, we need to "Wake up, America." We eat too much, exercise too little, and allow tension to tighten our nerves like banjo strings. All this adds up to hypertension and high blood pressure and makes us candidates for heart problems and strokes. *And it does not have to be this way!* That's the good news. It remains to be seen whether we will do anything about it, but we could if we would! This reminds me of the old saying, "I could if I would, but I can't *would*." Again, motivation is the key.

Business Realizes the Importance of Fitness

An increasing number of businesses are installing gymnasiums and jogging tracks and giving memberships to health clubs and the like. They are tired of pre-retirement disability, premature sickness, and accidents related to sluggishness and exhaustion. It is estimated that businesses in the United States lose twenty-five million dollars yearly because of early deaths, which are caused mostly by heart problems. Top business executives have come to expect physical fitness programs, and an increasing number of companies want their key employees attending Positive Thinking Seminars.

It follows that the worker who is physically fit and positive in his thinking will do a better job, produce more business, and is likely to be worth much more to himself, his family, and his company for a longer period of time. Why, then, do we fight such programs and resist all efforts to get us into shape? Basically, it's because we are just plain lazy. I'd call it a nicer term, if there was one, but you and I know that it's the truth.

My Story

As a minister of one of the fastest growing churches in the nation, I lead a busy life. I speak approximately 300 times a year and take probably thirty airplane trips annually. On the local scene, I have a heavy schedule of sermons and classes, a full calendar of counselling, a paper mountain of correspondence, and the many other details involved in a growing church.

A few years back, after I had taken 59 trips to speak on seminars around the country, I literally had preached my voice out. I developed a polyp on my vocal chords, and my blood pressure became quite high and erratic. My doctor told me I was on a collision course for a stroke or heart attack.

He put me in the hospital and made all those tests, hunting the "bad things" (tumor, etc.). Finally he looked at me, shrugged his shoulders and said, "Occupational hazard." Well that made me about half-mad. Here I am a gospel preacher, and I preach on love, joy, and peace, yet I am high strung, my nerves taut, and I'm a candidate for a heart attack! It just isn't right! And it *isn't,* my friend, for me or for you!

Jogging!

I have always been somewhat athletically inclined. I like to keep active in outdoor sports. So I thought, "I'll whip myself into shape and get up to running a mile or so each day." I reasoned that the exercise would keep me in shape so I could handle all the travel and pressures.

Well I was doing just fine at jogging. As a matter of fact, I was up to about two miles a day, and then our youth minister ruined me! He gave me a copy of *The Complete Book of Running,* by James Fixx. It turned my whole life around in a single day. I got really excited about running. Pretty soon, primarily motivated by that book, I was running three miles a day and then four. I set some goals. I would run 6 miles before summer, and on August 28, I would run 10 miles, non-stop.

Now I want to throw in a word of caution. Fixx's book instructs you to "listen to your body." I think that's one thing that turned me on. If your body hurts, slow down, or stop all together. Overexertion is not where it's at. And in your pre-run stretches, you "go to the limit of comfort." Now, you have to admit, that's a far cry from the old

Air Force days when they drove you to the point of dropping. But by following these easy instructions, before long I was running more, enjoying it more, and on August 28, 1978, I ran and completed that 10-mile run. Can you imagine what that did to my attitude?

Amazing Side Benefits

Well I went back to my doctor for a routine annual physical. He said, "Marvin, I don't know what you're doing, but your blood pressure is back to normal. I'm going to take you off medication." And that's somewhat rare, folks. Anyway, I've been off medication for almost four years, and I've never felt better in my life.

Let's count up the benefits of my fitness program: my blood pressure is normal, my chances of a heart attack are estimated at 64% less than a non-runner, and my 49 year old body is leaned down (153 pounds). I have never felt better in my life. I feel more mentally alert, and I am able to do more. And best yet, problems and pressures just don't get to me like they did before. I'm busier than ever, yet I handle it better than ever. Does this sound like something you can use? See your doctor (especially one who jogs and is skinny) and get started.

Practical Pointers

1. *Get your attitude right.* A good friend, who is a medical doctor, told me that he estimated

that 80% of all his patients complain of psychoso-
matic illnesses. That simply means, dear friends,
that illness is often caused by attitudes or emo-
tions, and not by physical problems. Clear up your
thinking, clean out your mind, and you'll be a
healthier person. Remember, "As a man thinks
in his heart, so is he" (Prov. 23:7). Put another
way, "Your life becomes what your mind is fed."

2. *Diet.* I'm not a dietitian, but you can find
one who will recommend a sensible approach. Your
body needs certain things, and you must get them.
Most of us eat too much, and we eat the wrong
things. We literally dig our graves with our teeth.
You wouldn't pour swamp water into your car's
gas tank (even in these days of $1.50 per gallon
gasoline); so don't put junk food into your valuable
body. It's the only one you've got, neighbor. Treat
it right!

3. *Sleep.* Get enough sleep, but most of us don't
need as much sleep as we suppose. I get along
just fine on 6 hours per night. I find that any
more than that doesn't help me at all. Learn to
sleep relaxed. Don't take tomorrow's troubles to
bed with you tonight.

Rise early! Get up before dawn. That's the most
beautiful time of the day. The world is clean and
beautiful. Being up early is wonderful for your
attitude.

You say, "I just *can't* get up early! And I'm a
bear in the morning." Well let's see if you really
are. Suppose I offer you $500 to wake up at 6:30
tomorrow morning, bounce out of bed and say,
"Boy do I feel *great!*" Could you do it? Of course

you could. In fact, you probably wouldn't sleep all night just thinking about it and waiting to do it for the $500. Well here's what we've found out. You *can* do it if the motivation is right! Now, all we have to do is to convince you that a healthy attitude and a vibrantly alive body and mind are worth more than $500.

4. *Exercise.* Some people enjoy jogging, while others prefer something else. Do whatever exercise you like, as long as it gets you into shape. How about cycling, hiking, swimming. Or, maybe you prefer tennis, racquetball, basketball, etc. Grab up Ken Cooper's book, *Aerobics,* or *Aerobics for Women.* These books are good, sensible, and easily within your ability. You're not in competition with anyone but yourself. And I can tell you, you're in for a lot of fun. It will add years to your life and life to your years!

Spiritual Fitness

Some people have never discovered how practical the Bible is. On physical fitness it says, "your body is the temple of God; don't destroy it" (1 Cor. 3:16). "Glorify God with your body and spirit" (1 Cor. 6:19–20). "I discipline my body" (1 Cor. 9:27). And even Jesus "grew in wisdom and *stature* (that's physical fitness), and in favor with God and men" (that's attitude) (Luke 2:52).

But we are physical, emotional, moral, and spiritual. The only road to total happiness is to understand this and to feed each of these needs. Get fit in each of the four ways. If you work on one and neglect the other, you cannot be complete and whole. In fact, the Bible word "holiness" just means "whole-ness."

Honor God because you are his creation. Read his will (the Bible: your owner's manual). Meditate upon his goodness and pray regularly. You cannot possibly measure the good that will come into your life if you spend even 5 minutes a day alone with God contemplating your relationship with him.

Greatest Compliment in the Bible

In the little book of Third John (which has only one chapter), John says of his beloved friend, Gaius, "Dear friend, I pray that you may enjoy good health, and that all may go well with you, even as your soul is getting along well" (v. 2).

This verse shows that physical health is important. It shows that wealth and success are important too. It shows that the most important of all is that our "souls prosper." Gaius was doing so well spiritually that John wished he might also do as well in the other two areas of his life. This physical, financial, and spiritual well being might well be called "the well-rounded life." Try it; you'll like it!

CHAPTER TWELVE

Associate with Winners

"Bad company corrupts good character" (1 Cor. 15:33).

If you want to set goals and reach them, you'll want to pay particular attention to this chapter. We've all heard the expressions, "you are known by the company you keep," and "birds of a feather flock together." It is really more than that. The people you choose to associate with will either be a positive force or a burden to you. That is, they will either help you along to the achievement of your goals or they will be a hindrance.

You will find that successful people associate with winners. On a recent flight I got absorbed in an article in *Inflight Magazine*. It was all about top executives under age 30 who were trying to find a pattern in their behavior or lifestyles. One thing stuck out! They all made contacts with top people. They made it a point to personally meet top people whenever possible and to listen to what they had to say.

We've Got to Study Successes!

If you are going to open up a hamburger stand, you don't want to talk with the owner of "Jake's Greasy Spoon." If he knew anything at all or had any ambition or drive, he wouldn't be in that dingy little place. You want to study the leaders. You want to get acquainted with MacDonalds, Burger King, Burger Chef, and businesses of that stature.

It works that way in building great churches too. I remember a few years back when I went to a small town to speak on "Effective Bus Ministry." Just before I got up to speak, the local preacher confided in me, "I don't believe in bus ministry." That blew me right out of the saddle. Where I preach, we run 33 buses and bring in 800 to 1,000 kids each Sunday. I said, "What do you mean, you don't believe in bus ministry?" And he said, "Well, I've been watching around. I know a church up the road that bought a bus. It is now sitting on their parking lot useless. The air is out of the tires, the motor is rusting, and the windows are broken. They bought a bus, and it didn't work. I don't believe in bus ministry."

I shot back, "I know a church that hired a preacher, and that didn't work either. I don't believe in hiring preachers."

You see, friends, we make a grave mistake in life when we study failures, because it gives us an excuse never to try. We can always find someone who has tried it and failed, but if you really want to succeed, go find a winner. Study him closely.

Do what he did, and you can accomplish what he accomplished.

In sports, play with someone just as good as you are, or perhaps a little better. That way you'll always learn something and be pushed to your maximum.

In church work, go where they are excelling. Go where the people come in large numbers, where they are excited, where their lives are changed, and where you can see the effect of the product on the "consumer." You'll never be motivated by hanging around mediocrity!

Not "Isolation," But "Insulation"

Now we don't mean that you must have absolutely no company with non-winners. The Bible reminds us that if we avoid bad folks altogether, we'd have to leave the world (1 Cor. 5:10). It just means that we should not allow them the position of influencing us to live as they live.

I'm reminded of the folks who won't go to church because there are hypocrites there. Now friend, there are hypocrites in the grocery business, but you keep eating. Some hypocrites sell gasoline, but you keep driving. And if you're of the opinion you're too good to associate with them, you just come along anyway, "one more won't hurt." In fact, maybe it's better to come on to church and have to rub elbows with a few hypocrites than to stay away and have to spend an entire eternity with all of them!

Anyway, "insulation" means to surround yourself with the right kind of influence. This applies to people, books, tapes, movies, events . . . well it applies to just about everything. You're finally going to become what you associate with! It's like the sign I heard about at the beginning of a long, muddy, country road. The sign read, "Choose carefully the ruts you enter; you'll be in them for the next 20 miles."

Make it a point to choose friends who are positive in their thinking. Read only the books that build you up and inspire you to do your best. Choose carefully the places you go and the events you watch. All of these have a profound effect on you.

Cassette Recordings . . . Spaced Repetition

When you attend Positive Thinking Seminars (and I hope you attend at least one each year), you'll hear a lot about cassette recordings and "spaced repetition." This is really the cassette age. Almost everyone has a cassette recorder. One of the most exciting marks of our generation is that so many are listening to motivational recordings in their cars, in their homes, and even when they jog.

It is a proven fact, that after you've heard the same recording seven times, you begin to think like what you've been listening to. I know personally that this is so. I discovered that I don't shave with my ears. So with my ears free while I shave, I always listen to cassette recordings. I have one in my little truck so I can listen during the 11 miles between my house and the church building. It is estimated that we spend 3 ½ years of our lives in our automobile. What an opportunity to pour good positive cassette recordings into your mind.

You'll pick up information each time you listen, up to over a dozen times, and inspiration unlimited times. I have just about worn out my set of Zig Ziglar's "How to Stay Motivated," and Norman Vincent Peale's, "Listen to Life." I have dozens more that are worth their weight in gold to me.

But I Can't Afford It!

Many people, even in this luxurious United States, still hang on to the old saying, "It costs too much." Now friend, cost is relative. If you don't spend money to send your kids to a good Christian summer camp, if you don't buy good books for your children to read and good cassettes to listen to; who knows, you may one day spend a lot more than that on lawyers' fees, hospital bills, and a mountain of other expenses.

The same applies to yourself. The pittance you spend for good motivational cassettes and books will be but a token compared to the actual dollars you'll earn, and the enjoyment of life you'll get by learning to think right. And who can measure the value of a solid marriage, a rewarding job, good kids, and a home in heaven?

In friends, books, and everything else, pick out some winners and associate with them. Let them help you to success and happiness!

CHAPTER THIRTEEN

I'm Partial to Thumbs

I have a bunch of dumb sayings that don't have any meaning at all. One my elderly stepfather likes best is, "Wherever you go, there you are. Whereas on the other hand, you have four fingers and a thumb." He likes it. It doesn't mean a thing, but he keeps asking me to repeat it.

But take a look at that hand again. Sure enough, it does have four fingers and a thumb, and there is quite a lesson there. There really are four fingers, and they all look pretty much alike, right? Same number of joints, and all about the same length. Then there's that dumb thumb stuck off to one side. It doesn't even look like it belongs there. And if fingers could talk they would probably say, "He's different. He doesn't belong with us. He's just an oddball." And we all join in castigating those poor thumbs. When we feel clumsy, we say, "I'm all thumbs." Poor thumb!

But without that thumb we'd be in a mess. We wouldn't have any grip at all. In Old Testament days they used to take captured warriors and cut off their thumbs and big toes (Judges 7). You see, that way they couldn't hold a sword or move around much in hand to hand combat.

Without that thumb, you'd have to learn a new way to hold a pen to write and a new way to do sign language. You couldn't throw a football or hitch a ride; you couldn't even thumb your nose at anybody.

Some of You Are "Thumbs"!

Some of you feel just about like that thumb. You feel slightly different from the rest and stuck off to one side. You are about to excuse yourself from excellence on account of it, and I'm about to take that excuse away from you. You see, it isn't fatal to be a thumb. It may not even be a disadvantage!

Thumbs Are Valuable

My thumbs are not for sale, not for $100,000 each. And if I didn't have any thumbs, that would be the first thing you'd notice about me. So if you accept me and love me, you've got to accept me "thumbs and all." They come with the package. To show this value, I'm going to give you a rather lengthy reading from 1 Corinthians chapter twelve (New International Version):

Now the body is not made up of one part, but of many. If the foot should say, "because I am not a hand, I do not belong to the body," it would not for that reason cease to be a part of the body. And if the ear should say, "because I'm not an eye, I do not belong to the body," it would not for that reason cease to be part of the body. If the whole body were an eye, where would the sense of hearing be? If the whole body were an ear, where would the sense of smell be? But in fact God has arranged the parts in the body, every one of them, just as He wanted them to be. If they were all one part, where would the body be? As it is, there are many parts, but one body (vs. 14–20).

I want to suggest that you read this Scripture over and over again until it dawns on you that the Lord isn't talking about a physical body at all. He's talking about the fact that we are all needed. We all have worth. We've been exclusively designed for a specific purpose. We don't need to be like anyone else. We need to "bloom where we're planted."

Lots of "Thumbs" Turn Out All Right!

In my ministry, I never cease to be amazed at the kids who turn out all right but who weren't raised as I teach people to raise kids. That's because "thumbs" do have that amazing capacity to turn out all right.

There were some great "thumbs" in the Bible. The apostle Peter was a thumb. He was always the first to speak, often with his "foot in his mouth." When Jesus told his disciples that they would forsake him and flee when trouble came, Peter corrected the Lord. "Though all men forsake you, I never will." Ah, but Peter was a "thumb." Later when Judas came with the mob to capture Jesus, the disciples all forsook him, and "Peter followed afar off." At the trial, several people accused Peter of being one of Jesus' disciples. But he cursed and swore, denying any knowledge of "this man." That fateful rooster crowed (as Jesus had promised), and Peter went out and wept bitterly.

But isn't it a marvelous story how this "thumb" made a comeback. Seven weeks later he was chosen to preach the first gospel sermon. Peter took the gospel first to the Gentiles. The first half of the book of Acts tells of his heroic work for Jesus. Two epistles in the New Testament bear his name. He was a "thumb" all right, and he proves to us that thumbs can make it!

Contemporary Thumbs!

I refer to those who, for one reason or another, were thought to be incapable of making it. A few years back, an incredible young lady from California made running history across our nation despite her epilepsy. We've spoken of Tom Dempsey, who made it to the top in pro football despite having only one hand and no toes on his kicking foot. The world is full of these "thumbs" who refused to be put on the shelf of mediocrity.

Our second son, Mark, is a "thumb." He was the fateful middle child and lived up to the reputation. He was accident prone all through school. While many kids break one collar bone during early years in school, Mark broke both! He was seldom without a cut, break, bruise, or scratch. He was a poor student in school and often thought he'd join the army because he didn't consider himself college material. I heard him describe himself as a "droopy eyed, scar-on-the lip, big lips" kid.

But you know that "thumb" did go to college. He applied himself, made good grades, did well with his fellow students, and graduated. He is now a highly successful minister. He's in constant demand as a speaker and does an impressive work.

Son-of-a-Thumb!

Mark is also the son of a thumb! You see, the reason I'm partial to thumbs is because "I are one!" From early years I could be described as having no self confidence, a low self image, no guts, fearful, bashful, mediocre in sports . . . a real "non-achiever"!

Even when I began to preach, I preached in small, out-of-the-way places. No one got excited over Marvin Phillips. I even moved to Australia, 11,000 miles from home, where the whole brotherhood could forget all about me.

The "Thumb" Comes to Tulsa

But a small group started a new church in a high school in Tulsa. Through the providence of God, they asked me to move there and preach for them. I came to a 91-member church in 1970, and from then on, my head is dizzy! God has allowed this "thumb" to be a part of the largest church of Christ in Oklahoma and the sixth largest in the world. I get asked to speak on major church growth clinics, seminars, and workshops all over the nation. I doubt if there is a man in our brotherhood who travels more than I do and speaks more times in a given year. No special ability! No logical explanation! I'm just a thumb! But God can use thumbs, if those thumbs are willing to place themselves in his hands.

This "thumb" now gets to appear on Positive Thinking Rallies, with such notables as Norman Vincent Peale, Robert Schuller, Zig Ziglar, Paul Harvey, Cavett Roberts, and others. The "thumb" is heard on cassette recordings and now the "thumb" has written a book.

Are you just a "thumb," my good friend? Never under-estimate the value and potential of a "thumb." Don't fret over what you don't have; just add up what you do have. It is enough if you apply it hard enough, long enough, and toward a worthwhile goal.

CHAPTER FOURTEEN

Feeling Good by Doing Right

Everybody seems to want to feel good; but either we don't know how, or after finding out how, we just won't pay the price! We live in a "if-it-feels-good-do-it; if-it-hurts-let-it-alone" world! Everybody wants to "do his own thing," yet this feeling of well-being is escaping far too many of us. Our mental institutions are full, and millions of tranquilizers are dispensed regularly—which attests to the fact that "somebody ain't feeling good."

"We Don't Feel Like It"

There are things we all want to do, "when we feel like it." We're going to conquer that bad habit. We will enrich our marriage. We will work on our relationship with our kids, our mate, our friends, our God. But we'll do all of this when the feeling is right! We'll start a savings account, get a physical, become a Christian, make an apology, get involved in our church "when we feel like it." But somehow, we never feel like it!

Some Things Never Feel Good!

An operation never feels good. Your doctor tells you you must have an operation. You never ask,

"Will it feel good?" do you? You never say, "I'll have it when I'm in the mood for an operation." Now, when in the world would anybody be in the mood for pain? "Doctor, will it hurt?" Of course it's going to hurt, and it's going to cost money. You will be incapacitated for a few days and have a long recovery period. Then why should I go through with it? Here's a couple of good reasons. You're going to die if you don't! And after recovery, you'll feel better than you have in years. Okay, doctor, I'll have the operation.

Now, man, if we could just think that way about life.

We have a lady in our church who has lost almost 70 pounds. I say, "Linda, was it fun losing all that weight?" and she replies, "No, it was misery! You can't believe the pain, the agony, and the temptation to eat sweets and fattening foods." Then why on earth did she do it, and what did she gain?

She knew she would die if she didn't lose weight! She was a prime candidate for a heart attack! So she did "right"! She worked at it. There was a price to be paid! And now she's a trim "109" (and that's her nickname, too). She feels good, and it came from doing right!

What About Your Bad Habits?

Have you realized you should quit drinking? Do you smoke cigarettes that say on the label "The Surgeon General Has Ruled That Cigarette Smoking is Hazardous to your Health"? You've been coughing a lot lately and want to quit? Do you need to break off an affair? I've got news for you, friend. It is never going to feel good to do it! But then, the alternative isn't so hot either. You can keep right on and head for the "marble orchard."

Marriage and "Good Feeling"

Having a great relationship with your mate and kids doesn't come without sacrifice! There are no accidentally happy marriages and no good relationships with the kids that are the result of fate. You've got to do the right things. Day after day, you've got to shoulder responsibility, maintain discipline, pour your time and your very life into it. It is often grueling and many times disappointing. But the end result is the great feeling of having a terrific marriage and kids that grow up and amount to something. Feeling good comes from doing right.

The Christian's "Good Feeling"

The Bible says Jesus came that we might have "life, and have it to the full" (John 10:10). But it isn't a better-felt-than-told thing. It doesn't strike you like lightning from the sky. At least that's not my experience. It comes from doing what's right.

Let me give you a case in point. In the book of Acts there are seven stories about how folks became Christians. In the eighth chapter you read about a government official from Ethiopia who became a Christian. The story ends with these word's, "and he went on his way rejoicing" (Acts 8:39). Now he wasn't struck with a lightning bolt.

Here's what happened (vs. 26–39). He was reading Scripture from Isaiah. The preacher (Philip) came along and taught him about Jesus. The man came to realize that Jesus was the Messiah (Saviour) that prophets had said would come into the world to save them. He found out Jesus died for him, was buried, and rose again. He heard that Jesus would come again some day to receive all those who trusted and obeyed him.

This caused the man to ask that they stop his chariot beside a pool of water. He was baptized into Christ and came up out of that water a new man. He had done right! That's why the Bible naturally concludes with, "and he went on his way rejoicing." I'm saying, "feeling good comes from doing right."

Now How About You?

Would you say your life is happy? Do you feel good about your job, your marriage, your kids, and your God? If not, I suggest that you search your life to see if you're "doing right." Feeling good comes from doing right, and the good thing is that you can start right now!

CHAPTER FIFTEEN

Learning the Skill of Positive Thinking

Basically, there are only two kinds of people in the world. There are the positive thinkers and the negative thinkers. The positive thinkers enjoy life, see the opportunities, and achieve the goals. The negative thinkers cop out. They "would have made it," except for the "system" (whatever that means). They are full of excuses. They had the wrong parents, were brought up in the wrong circumstances, or even were "born under the wrong star."

It is attitude more than circumstances that places the smile on the radiant countenance or the frown on the furrowed brow. It is simply amazing how you can get different responses from folks in the same circumstances.

For instance, the weather in a given place is exactly alike for all of us. Yet you say to one person "nice day isn't it." He replies, "It's a beauty!" Another person, experiencing exactly the same day, will say, "Well you know the old saying 'the calm before the storm.'" You can ask one man, "how're you doing?" He'll reply, "Great! Things are really going super." Ask another, and he'll say, "I think America is doomed unless we can get another President!" The world is drawn to the positive thinker; it is repelled by the negative thinker.

Positive Thinkers Are Made Not Born

Someone will say, "I'm just not a natural born positive thinker." Isn't it strange that some folks believe that the way you think is the result of birth? Friend, where, when, and to whom you were born has precious little to do with your attitude. Now your past may "explain" you, but it certainly doesn't lock you in. We are by choice, skill, and training what we are today! If you don't like it, change it! Someone says, "You can't teach an old dog new tricks." It's a good thing we're not dogs, isn't it!?

The Psalmist David

When most people think of David, the writer of the psalms, they think of the guy who walked so close to God. But David wasn't always that way. He led a miserable life until he learned the proper way to think and to act.

David may have said, "My wife doesn't understand me." So he got other wives. He had so many, he could go to bed with a different one every night; but it didn't satisfy. He saw Bathsheba. "Now there's the one I *really* want," he said. He had to have her husband killed to have her, but that was no problem for a king.

But it brought no happiness. He was a miserable, guilt-ridden man. God sent Nathan, the prophet, to convict David of his sin. He wrote psalm 51 while under this conviction. It is a miserable treatise. "My sin is ever before me," he cried.

But David repented of his sin, turned to God, and found the joy of living right again. After that he could write:

The Lord is my Shepherd, I shall not want,
He makes me to lie down in green pastures,
He leadeth me beside the still waters, He restores
   my soul.
He leads me in paths of righteousness for His
   names' sake.
Yea, though I walk through the valley of the
   shadow of death,
I will fear no evil, for you are with me;
Your rod and your staff they comfort me.
You prepare a table before me in the presence of
   my enemies.
You anoint my head with oil; my cup runs over,
Surely goodness and mercy shall follow me all the
   days of my life,
And I will dwell in the house of the Lord forever!
(Psa. 23).

We Live in a Negative World

We constantly have to fight off the negative garbage we hear every day. I told someone recently of a friend who was to have heart bypass surgery. His first comment was "I knew someone who had that surgery. He died on the operating table." Well I'm sure some do. But what I really wanted to hear was the possibility of good. How about the successful surgeries? How about the guys who recover and never felt better in their lives? That's what I wanted to hear! Incidentally, my friend had successful surgery, and is doing great! I can't wait to use him the next time someone tells me of a friend facing the same ordeal.

I've been thinking of collecting newspaper clippings so I can draw some bizarre conclusions. How about this one, "Man killed on motorcycle." Conclusion? Don't ride motorcycles. "Air crash claims 80." Conclusion? Don't fly in airplanes! "TWA flight barrelrolls." Don't fly TWA! "Jogger has heart attack." Don't jog! "Man shot by wife." Don't get married! Or this one, "Man has heart attack while making love." Conclusion? No Sex!

Look, there are guys who ride motorcycles, fly airplanes, jog, get married, and make love who enjoy it all immensely. Why take the unusual and make it the expected? I just don't choose to think negatively.

Want to Learn Positive Thinking?

1. *Learn to "believe."* Belief is the greatest healer in the world. Believe in yourself. Believe in the outcome. Say loudly to yourself several times each day, "I've got what it takes. God and I can handle anything."

2. *Learn to think.* When misfortune hits, don't get all gloomy and give up. Think positively.

There's got to be an answer. There must be a way. Agonize! Think deep! An answer will come. Make the decision, believing in the outcome. There is a solution to every problem. But we have to learn to think in order to find it!

3. *Learn enthusiasm.* When I look over my audience, one person often stands out as enthusiastic. Just look at that smile on his face. One fellow told me, "smiling won't solve anything; but it makes folks wonder what you've been up to." If you wake up in the morning moaning about "this is going to be another tough day," you have just locked it in so it *will* be a tough day! But start the day off with a little enthusiasm and watch the chips fly as you make positive things happen.

4. *Learn to pray.* How are you going to get anywhere in life if you don't talk to the Lord? He made you and wants you to succeed! He knows how you can succeed. He wrote a book about it. It's called "Holy Bible." Talk to the Lord through prayer, let him talk to you through the Bible. Here's a good prayer to start your day: "This is the day the Lord has made; I will rejoice and be glad in it" (Psa. 118:24).

You Can Do It!

Friend, you can be a positive thinker if you want to be. No one can take your optimistic view of life from you without your permission. It helps you see opportunity. Positive action makes it into reality. Know that you can, if you will it to be. . . . Get after it!

CHAPTER SIXTEEN

The Great Brain Robbery

Man originally had self-esteem. God made him that way. But somewhere along the way somebody robbed us of this valuable gift, and this has left us with a great feeling of inadequacy. We fear we "just don't have what it takes." What can we do about this robbery? And how can we get back what we lost?

Atheists Are "Made," Not "Born"

There are some things we know naturally. For example, babies know they've got mamas, and they will cry 'til at her breast. They soon learn that toys have makers, and they come to understand that somewhere there is a man who loves little children. He designs and manufactures toys to please them, to make money, and therefore to pay his bills. As they grow older they come to realize that everything has a builder or an origin! They know that houses prove that there are house-builders. And finally it dawns on them that a world demands and proves a world-maker. The sun, moon, stars, flowers, animals, and yes, man himself, proves that there is a Maker behind it all.

While these babies are still "brand new," they possess all the qualities they need to make it in life, to set and reach goals, and to find happiness and success.

They are alert! You seldom see a dull, lethargic baby. They are by nature enthusiastic. They want "in" everything; they want to be included in everything. And they are trusting. You never saw a suspicious, grudging, and inhibited baby. And babies really believe! They are not agnostic. They are confident they can do anything in the world. They are honest! Later, they learn from negative thinkers to be conniving, flattering, and politicking! And they are loving! They love people, plants, and animals (even fuzzy, slimy ones). They will love anything or anyone that will let them. In fact, they can win over the hearts of the most hardened with that genuine, unpretended love.

These are the qualities we need today to help us cope with life. They are the characteristics that will help us succeed. We had them when we were born, then somehow they were stolen from us. How did it happen, and what can we do about it?

Scientific Discovery Dwarfed Us!

You see, originally man believed he was special, and this is the way every baby feels. Children naturally feel close to God; they are easily taught to pray, to love, to share. They feel superior to all animals, and are not intimidated by anything.

Then we found out that we are just a speck on a speck in a universe composed of millions of galaxies like our own. We learned that our earth was 8,000 miles thick and 25,000 miles around. We sent a man to the moon and measured the distance to other planets. Each of these discoveries, while thrilling and exciting, dwarfed man's size. Many of us feel so small and insignificant, that we lose our self-worth.

What we forget is that when God made this gigantic universe, He said, "Let's give man dominion over all we've made" (Gen. 1:28). We are the biggest thing in the universe. There never will be a planet of the apes with insects taking over. That will have to remain science fiction. Man is in control. And we are the only thing that exists that is made "in the Image of God." I'm feeling better already. I hope you are too.

Theory of Evolution Robbed Us!

Then man got another blow to his self-worth. Not only did he learn that he is a speck, but that he evolved from an ape. And God only knows what he was before that—so teaches evolution. Now, the most important thing you can learn about evolution is that it is a "theory," not a fact! There are folks who believe that science has "proven" evolution. If so, which theory did they prove, since there are over 26 different theories on evolution?

Here's another thing many people don't know. There is no known, proven, scientific fact that contradicts the Bible. Not one! "Well," I hear someone say, "The Bible says the earth is only 6,000 years old." Really? Where does the Bible say that? I've never found any verse in the Bible that hints at the age of the earth.

But I do know this: man "arrived"; he did not "survive" through a series of evolved species. Man never crosses lines of species (Gen. 1:21), nor is he an accident. He was designed on purpose for the special place of dominating the universe. You can go as high as you dream. Don't let evolutionary theory rob you of your importance and self-worth!

The Fickle Finger of Fate

The final straw that robs man of his individual choice, value, and potential is his belief in "fate." Dr. Freud came on the scene with his theory that man is unable to control his actions. You are a helpless victim of Aunt Polly's genes, or horse-thief ancestors. We are asked to believe that some people are born to be good and that much bad conduct was already decided by heredity!

And that's where the "horror-scope" comes in. Americans read that thing daily, and laugh, but far too many believe that their fate and future is decided by their "sign." There's a Greek word for this. . . *baloney!* When an airplane crashes killing 200 people, doesn't it dawn on you that some died in that crash from every "house" in the zodiac?

Now the danger of this satanic influence is that we lose responsibility for our actions. If it has already been decided how we will act, we can now blame all our wrongs on something else. Having lost moral accountability and feeling powerless to take charge of our destinies, our self-esteem goes out the window. So, feeling we are no more than weeds in the garden, we now drink too much, drive too fast, eat the wrong foods, marry and divorce lightly, cop out, indulge; and in the process we destroy our potential and our future. We've been robbed, my friends. Let's get back what has been taken from us!

Reclaiming Our Sense of Value!

Someone says, "I'm just not worth anything. No one needs me. The world would be better off without me." They've lost their self-worth! How does one get it back?

If I told you that I recently bought a car and paid $50 for it, what would you think? What's your first thought? Is it, "Boy, Marvin is smart. Man, imagine getting a fantastic car for only $50"? Or does your mind conjure up a vision of a total wreck or a totaled-out junk heap"?

What if I asked you to come outside and see my new $30,000 automobile, what would you expect to see? Okay, am I right in assuming that you think my $50 car is a wreck? And did I guess right in assuming that you think I must have a brand new Mercedes Benz diesel if I paid $30,000?

Now what I'm getting at is this. Our mind registers value by the price paid. The higher the price, the higher the value. Now friend, what is your value?

If you've got a good marriage and good kids,

your family wants you more than they want to collect your $100,000 insurance. To them you are worth much more. Your friends and loved ones value you; some of them might even die for you if necessary.

The Cross Argues for My Worth

Read the golden text of the Bible, "For God so loved the world, that He gave His One and Only Son that whoever believes in Him shall not perish but have eternal life" (John 3:16). Now here's the point. You were being auctioned off between God and Satan. No matter how much Satan bid for you, God always raised it. Finally, God offered the price that Satan could not match. God gave his own son to die in your stead.

Now, my reading friend, there are some people in the world I believe I'd die for. But there is no one on earth I'd give one of my kids for. I can't understand God believing in me that much, but I appreciate it and love him for it. And my self-worth has just hit the sky. I am worth that much to God! To him, I am really somebody! Why not, then, live like it here on earth?

CHAPTER SEVENTEEN

To Get More, You Must Produce More

A man reaps what he sows (Gal. 6:7).

Years ago, while in the United States Air Force, I saw a leadership training film entitled, "To Get More, You Must Produce More." It reminded us of the simple fact that life is a "percentage game." You can plan on getting back in direct proportion to what you give. It works in any field and with anything!

The quickest and surest route to riches is commission selling. There is no ceiling on the salesman's salary. He can get a raise anytime he wants. He just makes more calls, puts out more effort, makes more sales, and the increase in salary is there.

Man as an individual is totally unpredictable; but in the masses, he is a sure thing. You could not possibly guess what a man will do next. But human nature is so predictable that insurance companies know how many will die on a given weekend and can set premium rates with such accuracy as to come out millions of dollars ahead.

Salesmen soon learn that "making calls" is all a matter of percentages. They may call it "prospecting" or "farming," but it works on the principle that if you contact enough people with your goods or services, you can have success.

Sowing and Reaping

The Bible says, "Do not be deceived: God cannot be mocked. A man reaps what he sows. The one who sows to please his sinful nature, from that nature will reap destruction; the one who sows to please the Spirit, from the Spirit will reap eternal life." Three principles emerge from the law of sowing and reaping.

1. *You will reap what you sow!* You cannot sow one thing and reap another. You can't plant watermelons and expect to reap peanuts. Seed will reproduce after its kind.

It reminds me of a story my mother used to tell me when I was a little boy. I enjoyed it and it taught a valuable lesson. It seems that a man found some buzzard eggs. His wife had an old setting hen and she hoped to soon have some baby chicks. Well, the man substituted those hen eggs for the buzzard eggs. He figured it would really be something when his wife discovered baby buzzards under her hen. Well a few days went by, and finally the man asked his wife, "Honey, have those eggs hatched yet?" And she replied, "Oh, I got tired of fooling with them and cooked them for your breakfast this morning." The Bible has a verse for this; "Be sure your sins will find you out" (Num. 32:23).

But the principle of reaping what you sow works in so many ways. What if you want to reap happiness, success, sales, a good marriage, or lots of friends. Well it means you're going to have to sow happiness. You'll have to think happy thoughts and talk happy things to everybody. You'll have to put a smile on your face. You'll have to act successful and imagine yourself as a success. You'll have to believe in a good marriage and provide for your mate's needs cheerfully and adequately. To have friends, you must be a friend! You reap what you sow!

2. *You reap more than you sow!* I once heard of a prosperous farmer up in Canada who had 2,500 acres of corn. Someone asked him how he happened to have so much corn! He replied jokingly, "Oh, you take a handful of corn, and walk through the field. Now and then you drop a grain here and there." And then he told the truth, "I've got a thirty-foot planter. I buy the best seed corn and plant it generously all over those 2,500 acres. The result is all that fine corn you see in my field."

You see friends, one kernel of corn grows a whole stalk with several ears of corn on it. If you plant a bean you'll reap a lot of beans. And so it is with life.

The Bible verse is, "whoever sows generously, will reap generously" (2 Cor. 9:6). If you share one smile, you will get a bunch of them back. Just being a friend, gets you a whole bunch of friends.

One kind deed nets much kindness toward your-self. One sale, cheerfully and honestly made, will net you many more customers. It has a snowballing effect. Yes, you reap *more* than you sow!

3. *You reap later than you sow!* Now this principle gets us into trouble. For we Americans want instant results! We pray, "Lord give me patience, and give it to me *right now!*" I heard about a sign on the highway, "Antiques Manufactured While You Wait." Ours is the age of instant coffee and instant divorce. We turn the lights on in the hen-house to fool the chickens into laying more eggs. We play soft music to cows to make them give "contented milk." In some things this might work, but generally you reap later than you sow.

That's what makes Zig Ziglar's pump story so effective. You know that if you grab onto the handle and pump long enough, it is a foregone conclusion that you will get more water than you can drink. Results in life come to the fellow who keeps pumping!

Quality of Life

"Give, and it will be given to you. A good measure, pressed down, shaken together and running over, will be poured into your lap. For with the measure you use, it will be measured to you" (Luke 6:38). My, my, can't we use this in our many pursuits of life?

Do you want more money? Do you want more of the material things of life? Great! Then learn to give more! John D. Rockefeller has this philosophy; take your prosperity and give away a third, keep a third for yourself, and invest a third. You may doubt the power of this, but this powerful family-clan has used this philosophy to amass a fortune for themselves.

If you study human needs and wants, and supply those needs honestly, cheerfully, and dependably, you will have all the material success you can handle!

Would you like to enrich your marriage? What are you *giving?* Do you supply your mate's needs? Do you study the needs of your children, and try to meet them? It's not money we're talking about. Do you give of yourself? Our problem is we have it backward. We want reward first! But it doesn't work that way. You treat me better, and then I'll treat you better! But any good salesman knows (and we are all salesmen) the reward comes after the hard work, and it comes in large proportions to make the effort worth the reward.

It Works in Building a Great Church

Robert Schuller's statement is so true: "Find the hurt in the community and heal it." This is why the Garnett Road Church of Christ is growing. We are people-oriented, and we'd do almost anything to help them. If they are unhappy, we'll try to give them happiness. If they are suffering, we'll try to give them comfort. If they've lost their way, lost their marriages, lost their health, we'll try to heal their wounds. Jesus died to help people who are lost in sin, and we want to help them to salvation. It's as simple as that. Meeting peoples' needs will get you out of the "church business" and into the "people business." Jesus died for people! The process of "sowing and reaping" is never more effective than in building a great church in your community.

Your Choice!

Here's what's good about the process of "sowing and reaping." It is all up to you. You can choose what you sow and when to sow it. You can also choose how much to sow. But after these choices are made, you are bound to the law of consequence. You'll reap *what* you sow, you'll reap *more* than you sow, and you'll reap *later* than you sow.

And here's a closing sentence that will get you going. It only has 10 words, twenty letters in all. *"If it is to be, it is up to me."*

CHAPTER EIGHTEEN

The Need for Praise

"You don't bring me flowers anymore." These are more than the words to a song, they are sadly a "way of life" for too many people. We take our loved ones for granted. We fail to compliment and praise them, and then we wonder, in our loneliness, how it all went wrong.

A little praise goes a long way. You can literally praise your marriage into greatness. You can praise your kids into success. You can praise your business, your customers, your employees, even your boss into greatness! Praise helps our self-esteem. It is the best preventive medicine in the world. It is better than a whole drug store full of prescriptions.

The Bible Spells out That Need

"Give her the reward she has earned, and let her works bring her praise at the city gate" (Prov. 31:31).

Jesus was quick with praise. When an army officer impressed Jesus with his faith, Jesus spoke out to all the crowd: "I tell you the truth. I have not found anyone in Israel with such great faith" (Matt. 8:10). Before a large audience, Jesus said of Nathaniel "Here is a true Israelite, in whom there is nothing false" (John 1:47).

The Scriptures are abundant with evidence that the disciples of Jesus learned the importance of praising others. Notice a few of Paul's sentences: "I commend to you our sister Phebe . . . she has been a great help to many people including me" (Rom. 16:1–3); "such men deserve recognition" (1 Cor. 16:18); "and we are sending along the brother who is praised by all the churches" (2 Cor. 8:18); "I have no one else like him" (Timothy) (Phil. 2:20). These are just a few of the praises and compliments given and shared publicly in the Bible. The writers must have thought it was important.

Praise Who?

Praise your loved ones at home. Some are pretty good at praising "away from home," but not so good at home. Friend, start at home. Praise your kids. Surely they do *something* right! Praise them for it. It might shock them to death, but do it anyway!

Be a complimenter, a "joy spreader." I found a choice retort I'm going to use the next time I hear someone cutting me down for some fault. "If my critic had known about all my other faults, he would not even have fooled around with that little one." Don't you like that? Why get all defensive? I know I'm not perfect, and I know I do the best

I can, so why should I fuss and fight with a critic? Someone has said, "There is so much good in the worst of us, and so much bad in the best of us, that it ill behooves any of us to speak evil of the rest of us." Hmmm!

Praise When?

Praise when you honestly can! Don't fake it! People hate nothing more than "gushy, insincere flattery." Try hard to find some honest area for praise. Maybe you'll be like the woman who was racking her brain trying to think of a compliment for her cantankerous husband. Finally she brightened up and said, "He breathes even." Well I hope you can find just a little something more than that to say!

Praise publicly! Criticize, if you must, in private, but praise openly. It will bring tremendous results!

Praise How?

Praise unconditionally—with no strings attached! Don't use praise just to get favors. Praise face to face, eye to eye. Perhaps with your hand on their shoulder. Or shake their hand vigorously, and with a smile, give that sincere praise that is deserved and that will mean so much.

Praise is a Two-Fold Blessing

Praise blesses the life of the one being praised. It will brighten his day, and lift his spirit. It will probably come at a time when he needs it most. Praise gives new direction and makes those who are discouraged want to try again. It will motivate them to excellence. You know exactly how it feels to hear praise, because it's the way you felt the last time someone praised you for a job well done.

Praise also blesses the life of the "praiser." You can't scatter sunshine without getting a generous portion on yourself. It will brighten your own outlook and cure your negativism. It will make you see today's opportunities in a different light. Yesterday you were a cynical, uptight, hard-to-get-along-with criticizer. Today you are praising everyone you see, about everything that is genuine. Why, shucks, you're having the time of your life! You just might do it again tomorrow. Better yet, this is the way you're going to live the rest of your life. Good for you.

While I'm at it, let me praise you a little. Thank you for buying this book. I hope it is a blessing to your life. And if you'll write me and tell me so, I'll answer. For you see, your letter will have brightened my life just a little. Hey, let's start a "praise epidemic" all across America.

CHAPTER NINETEEN

There is Always Hope

This is a golden age in which we live. Never have there been more opportunities for success and happiness than today. America truly is the land of the free and the land of opportunity. With our marvelous free enterprise system, you can accomplish almost anything you want.

In spite of this, there are many who feel "hopeless." They look hopeless and they talk hopeless. They believe they are hopeless, and they have the attitude of hopelessness. If jobs are mentioned, they don't have one or can't get one, and they have bills they can't pay. If debt is mentioned, they can't meet their obligations. They fear bankruptcy and have no credit. Concerning health, they are sick or are afraid of getting sick. Many are downcast. Some have been declared "terminal."

Many also feel their marriages are hopeless. They say they have fallen "out of love" with their spouse. They are separated, divorced, or deserted.

Many churches just exist. They are "keeping house" for the Lord, having lost sight of their purpose.

When we talk to folks about becoming Christians, many feel they have done too many bad things. They are drunkards or on drugs or immoral. They are into prostitution or in prison. So, for many, this book wouldn't mean much, because they feel they are "hopeless."

But There Is Always Hope

Even for the sick, there is hope. What an age we live in. Modern medicine changes overnight. New cures are constantly being found for old diseases. Folks used to die if they had tonsillitis or appendicitis; now you rarely even hear of these kinds of surgeries. Just around the corner there is a cure for cancer, Parkinson's disease and others.

And of course there's prayer. Prayer has wrought more wonders than this old world dreams of. Prayer might bring cure. It will certainly bring help to the sufferer.

You can learn to live with sickness even though you may be terminally ill. In my congregation we have a group of ladies who have been declared "terminal," and it is a real lift to my spirits to be around them. They are more radiant than many who are in sound physical health. In fact, if you'll write me, I'll put you in touch with them!

There's Hope for a Good Job

Do you really want a good job? America has the strange problem of having much unemployment, while the daily papers have page after page of "help wanted" advertisements. Ask any employer! "Would you hire an aggressive, honest, hard working person with a positive mental attitude?" He'll sigh, wishing he could find such people to hire. He'll tell you, "You can't believe the help you get nowadays." Well where do you find such people? Neighbor, that's you I'm describing, if you only choose to be this way.

In case you own your own business or want to start one of your own, just study the needs of people. You can get anything in life you want, if you'll just help enough other people get what they want! Humans are going to get what they want, and if you are willing to supply it with a positive mental attitude, they'll do business with you.

There's Hope for Your Marriage

Maybe your marriage needs "mouth-to-mouth resuscitation." Well, there's good news. You can pump new life into an old marriage. You and your mate can learn how to supply each other's needs. There are no "unsolveable problems" in a marriage, there are only people who won't try to solve problems.

Each year in Tulsa I do a three month's course called "Toward a Richer, Happier Marriage." We go to a neighborhood school each week for the one-hour sessions. There is no charge and it is open to the public. It makes for thirteen exciting Wednesday nights. If you're anywhere near Tulsa, attend this course. If not, write for the cassette album by that title. It is yours for a nominal fee.

But the point is: married happiness is a "skill" that anyone can learn. Life is just not all that complicated, but we often make it so by our selfishness and stubbornness.

Just understand that marriage is God's arrangement. He knows more about it than anyone, because he wrote a foolproof marriage manual called the "Holy Bible." Now friend, it makes no sense at all that God would make us as we are and then write a Bible that would inhibit our lives and keep us from happiness. As a matter of fact, perhaps you should scrape the gold letters off the front of your Bible, and put in their place, "Guide to Married Happiness," or maybe "Gusto Living Manual." It is certainly either of those.

There's Hope for Dead Churches

There is hope for dead churches, and I know churches that have been in a rut for years. A rut is just a grave with both ends knocked out. Church leaders need to rediscover what Jesus really meant when he promised to build his church on earth. He did not have a cold committee in mind who would wring their hands in horror while the rest of the world goes to Hell. The church is people, and it is in the "people business." It is not in the business of buildings, budgets, and buses! Not carpet, cooling, and committees! It is in the business of people!

Any church in the nation can be revived if it will rediscover its purpose and begin preaching the message of the Bible . . . the good news of

Jesus Christ. Many churches should quit conducting their worship like a funeral service. A worship service is many things: it is celebration of the risen Lord; it is a "Family Reunion" (notice all those Bible terms, "Child of God," "Father," "Born Again," etc.). When you think about it, all of these are down-to-earth terms. They spell out *"family."* When a church discovers the family spirit, it is on its way to greatness.

No One is Beyond Hope

I like the book of Corinthians. Paul gives a list of those who won't go to heaven. He says the sexually immoral, idolators, adulterers, male prostitutes, homosexual offenders, thieves, greedy, drunkards, slanderers, and swindlers won't make it. Then he proceeds to say, "and that is what some of *you* were." "Now," he says, "you are washed, sanctified, and justified" (1 Cor. 6:9–11).

Can you visualize this? Paul looks over the attendance of the church in Corinth and spots some in the audience who have been guilty of all the above named things. He smiles! Ah, it feels good to know how much the gospel can help people. Doctor's and lawyers sometimes have clients they can't help. But, you see, I never have to tell someone, "You've been too bad. You're beyond help." *There is always hope!* And where I preach, I get the same satisfaction. Name the sin, and somebody in that audience has been guilty of it. But thanks to an almighty God and a glorious gospel, they've been reached and changed, and their lives have been blessed. Perhaps that's why there's so much joy around this place!

The Relationship That Nothing Can Threaten

The spiritual relationship with God is ultimately the only thing that lasts. All else is temporary. Our houses will some day crumble, our cars and clothes will wear out, and our cash will finally desert us. Only the relationship with God is permanent and immortal: the stock market can't change it; germs and disease can't infect it; storms can't assail it; moods can't change it (Mal. 3:6); war can't invade and capture it; courtroom decisions can't take it away; misunderstandings won't make it go away; temptation and sin can't force it from us.

Final Verse

I suppose I'm groping for a Bible verse to sum up in a nutshell what I've been rambling on about. Perhaps this is it: "Physical training is of some value, but godliness has value for all things, holding promise for both the present life, and the life to come" (1 Tim. 4:8).

If only I've convinced you that you can have a super life now and a fantastic eternity later, these pages have not been in vain. With a prayer in my heart, these words pleadingly go out to you.

CHAPTER TWENTY

"For Christians Only!"

The things I've written in this book will work for anyone in any station in life. They will help you cope with life! But I want to add this last chapter especially for my believing friends.

Remember that little lady I told about in chapter one? She keeps haunting me because I see so many like her. Because they can't stay "up" spiritually, they feel they aren't cut out to be a Christian. Because of their human frailty, they eventually throw up their hands and throw in the towel. I want you to know the two most important things in your spiritual life.

Get Your Spiritual "New Start"

Jesus called it "being born again." That's the way you got into your physical family, and that's the way you get into God's family also. The three facts of the gospel (good news) are the death, burial, and resurrection of Jesus (1 Cor. 15:1–4)!

The first six verses of the sixth chapter of Romans tell you how you go through that birth process to start you on a brand new life. Like Jesus, you also have your own death, burial, and resurrection. When you die to sin (make a decision against it), you are buried with Christ in baptism, and coming from that grave of water you "walk in newness of life."

Your "Four Most Important Verses"

Now, to the Christian, 1 John 1:6–9 are the most important verses in the Bible. Let's take time to look at them;

"If we claim to have fellowship with him, yet walk in the darkness, we lie, and do not live by the truth (v. 6).

"But if we walk in the light, as he is in the light, we have fellowship with one another, and the blood of Jesus, his Son purifies us from every sin (v. 7).

"If we claim to be without sin, we deceive ourselves, and the truth is not in us (v. 8).

"If we confess our sins, he is faithful and just and will forgive us our sins, and purify us from all unrighteousness" (v. 9).

The "Marvin Phillips Translation"

The above verses from 1 John 1 are quoted from the New International Bible. Let me now put them in my own simple way!

Verse 6: God says, *"Don't play games with me."* He can see through them, and you don't need them. Don't think you've found a loophole by going to church on Sunday and then living like the Devil during the week.

Verse 7: *"Walk in the light; I'll keep you saved."* This scares us at first. We think it means "sinless perfection." So we don't think we can stay saved every day. To answer this Jesus says,

Verse 8: *"I know you have sin in your life."* This verse goes with verse 7. The two together must mean, "make a genuine commitment; a perfect commitment of an imperfect life." You are not saved because you are good; you are saved because He is good!

Yes, Lord, but what do I do about my sins?

Verse 9: *"Genuinely confess them to me:* I'll forgive them all." Now, good friend, you still have a choice. You can turn your back on God and be lost. These verses show how a stumbling, fumbling Christian can get to heaven, but he *doesn't fly there in a straight line!* We stumble, we stagger, we fall down. But because of our commitment to Jesus, he forgives when we ask him, and he will forgive *anything . . . anytime!*

Christian friends, get these four verses on straight, and your Christianity will become a delight. You'll know who you are, whose you are . . . and you'll know where you're going! *Happy landing!*